CORPORATE GOVERNANCE FROM STARTUP TO SCALE-UP

LUC STERCKX

CORPORATE GOVERNANCE FROM STARTUP TO SCALE-UP

Leuven University Press

ISBN 978 94 6270 424 4 (Paperback)
D/2024/1869/18
NUR: 780

Layout: Crius Group
Cover design: Frisco

CONTENTS

FOREWORD BY REGINALD VOSSEN

In this new book, Luc Sterckx once again strikes the right tone to convey the principles of corporate governance in an understandable manner to all those involved in setting up and nurturing young promising companies. The pitfalls—or are they excuses?—for not or not yet engaging with Corporate Governance effectively are often the same: lack of time, shortage of knowledge, fear of the unknown, fear of losing control, procrastination, etc.

That's precisely why it's important for someone to provide feasible guidelines to this target audience, thus lowering the barrier to at least getting started and gradually professionalizing from there. The fact that this author is an extremely experienced director and investor in growth companies only adds value to this publication. Drawing from his extensive experience, Luc once again provides perfect clarity on what works and what doesn't … As a member of BAN Flanders, Luc has already seen many entrepreneurs come and go, often sharing his insights with them and fellow business angels. All this results in a book that reads smoothly and comes across as very hands-on.

And just like the companies he advises, Luc also evolves in this new edition: while his previous publication focused solely on the world of startups, this new book explicitly broadens its scope to the scale-up phase as well. A new growth phase in a company inevitably brings new challenges in terms of corporate governance.

At BAN Flanders, we continue to support Luc Sterckx in his plea and the inclusion of all stakeholders in this endeavor. We are happy to convey his message because the implementation of corporate governance principles perfectly aligns with our vision of how "wise money" from business angels can be maximally efficiently deployed in sustainable deals.

Reginald Vossen
CEO BAN Business Angels Network Flanders

FOREWORD BY CLAIRE MUNCK

Instant successes are a mirage. For entrepreneurs, the path of development from startup to scale-up involves many ingredients for success: team alignment, recruitment and retainment of the best talent, advancement toward product/market fit, cash management and the management of successive funding rounds, etc. It further requires a strong shareholder base and the implementation of effective governance. As the CEO of BeAngels, as a board member of many companies, but also the founder and managing partner of the Scalefunds, investing in post-startup/pre–scale-up phases, I recognize the paramount importance of choosing the right board members and having an effective and supportive board in place. Starting up is one thing, successfully reaching the scale-up phase is not so easy. Unfortunately, corporate governance is often relegated to the bottom of the priority list by founders who are focused on building their team, their product, and reaching sales targets with satisfied customers. With so much to do, governance can seem like a burden rather than an opportunity. Having a good board and governance in place will make all a lot of these things easier; failing to communicate properly with the board and underestimating the value of good governance for existing and future shareholders can soon render all of the company's efforts useless. As an experienced director, with this new book Luc Sterckx once again draws attention to the economic impact of healthy corporate governance on start-ups and scale-ups, on existing and future directors and founders alike. A very useful read indeed!

Claire Munck
CEO BeAngels and Founder/Managing Partner Scalefunds

FOREWORD BY SANDRA GOBERT

It was a pleasure for GUBERNA's Centre of Expertise "SME Governance" to assist seasoned board member and loyal GUBERNA member Luc Sterckx with the updated version of his publication *Corporate Governance from Startup to Scale-Up*, addressing the sometimes neglected segment of small- and medium-sized companies.

We warmly applaud this initiative, which responds to a real need for starting companies with "agile" specificities.

At GUBERNA, the Belgian Institute of Directors, we believe in governance as an instrument of balanced decision-making. We plead for modern governance: a dynamic process in which "one size does not fit all" but in which governance is tailored to the type of company involved and evolves alongside the company's life cycle. As reflected in the work of GUBERNA's Centers of Expertise, there are different governance needs for different organizations: founder/entrepreneur, startup/scale-up, family business, partnerships, or ecosystems/cooperations.

Luc Sterckx' book is a pleasant and easy read and contains a lot of practical tips to get you started. The author uses his rich experience to show the way: he guides the reader not only through the "why" but also and especially through the "how."

There are basic principles to respect and choices to be made. Good governance is the key to the professional decision-making companies need on their path to growth.

Throughout his book, the author convincingly demonstrates that good governance has evolved to become much more than just some rules to abide by. This new version updates the principles of the previous one, with more references to the relevant experiences of the author. It also describes the evolution and necessary adjustments in corporate governance as the company scales up.

For GUBERNA, good governance indeed is a whole, consisting of the appropriate people, structures, and processes that help define a clear purpose for the organization and craft a sustainable strategy toward this purpose, stimulating entrepreneurship within ethical and legal boundaries.

We believe that better governance and better boards lead to better decisions and that better decisions contribute to a better world.

We are proud that our members spread this message, and we thank Luc Sterckx for being an outstanding ambassador of governance and an active contributor to our Centre of Expertise on SME Governance (https://www.guberna.be/en/know/organisation-types/centre-sme-governance).

Sandra Gobert
GUBERNA
Executive Director

PREFACE

In a previous book I covered the fascinating but also challenging world of startups in general and in particular the role Corporate Governance has to play in such environments.[1] Reflecting on my hands-on experience of the last decade in several startups, I have observed that governance should be adjusted as the startup evolves and changes.

It is safe to say that Corporate Governance is rarely a priority for startup companies. In such companies the number one job is often just to survive. However, I remain convinced the Corporate Governance is a must in any startup. Excuses such as "we are only a startup, we don't need all that stuff" and/or "we have so many other things to do urgently" are less valid than ever in the face of challenges the company will have to overcome.

In particular, one can often observe a kind of initial "grace period" where the starting capital, possibly complemented by subsidies, provides the startup with a comfortable platform to at least be financially worry-free for a couple of years. Unfortunately fairy tales do not last long, and after some time one finds the startup facing

1 Luc Sterckx, *Corporate Governance in Startups* (Leuven: Acco, 2020).

problems linked to growth financing, competitive pressure, internal disputes, and possibly even existential cash shortage issues.

Within this evolution, the transition to a scale-up is a process that requires particular skills and competencies, not in the least because it frequently involves additional capitals rounds. And while I have demonstrated before how much Corporate Governance is essential for any startup, I can only stress that it becomes even more important during a company's post-startup evolution.

The above conclusion is largely based on the numerous "living labs" I have had the good fortune of being involved in over more than a decade. I led a startup myself many years ago and have been directly involved in some twenty-five startups, in roles that have included several Board memberships and Chairmanships and shareholder / financial funder. Having now also gone through a number of scale-ups, I thought it may be useful to also share this experience and the lessons learned.

This book thus reflects some of my views on the matter and the intent to put them to good use for the many startups flourishing these days and trying to get to the next level of a scale-up. While readdressing and updating the essentials for Corporate Governance in startups, the book also covers the transition to scale-up and the consequences this entails for Corporate Governance in the evolving company landscape.

I am indebted to many people in completing this work: first of all to the Board Directors I had in my different CEO positions but also to my fellow Directors in the other Boards I have had the pleasure of sitting on. A special word of thanks goes to the teachers of GUBERNA and INSEAD where I perfected my knowledge of Corporate Governance and last but not least to the startups/

scale-ups I was active in recently and which allowed me to engage in a little "governance experimentation" now and then.

I extend thanks to the managers and Directors of the many startups I had the pleasure of cooperating with and their acceptance of me implementing some new approaches and ideas. My sincere appreciation also for the opportunities created by BAN Vlaanderen and BeAngels and other startup-stimulating organizations.

Davy Gorselé and Cédric Vaes from the team of Quorum have been kind enough to review this work from a legal point of view, for which I extend to them a word of special recognition.

A further big thank you to Prof. dr. Abigail Levrau for adding new perspectives and trends to this work.

To conclude, special thanks goes to GUBERNA and in particular to Sander Berghmans, Olivier Braet, and CEO Sandra Gobert for their professional input and interesting suggestions: they have contributed significantly to the quality of the publication.

Luc Sterckx
Brasschaat
January 2024

I dedicate this book to my eternally understanding spouse Christine, who once more had to share me with my professional occupation …

1

INTRODUCTION

Why this (new) book?

Corporate Governance has seen a considerable evolution and development over the last decades. Originating as an approach to avoid or handle mismanagement, abusive power, conflicts of interest, or fraud, it has gradually evolved to a more positive approach focusing not only on avoiding mishaps but also on stimulating the best possible performance of the structures it is supposed to cover and to govern.

One can equally see and understand that the initial target of Corporate Governance was the "bigger" companies, in particular ones listed publicly on the stock market. The obvious reason for this is that there was more at stake in these companies than in the smaller ones, specifically more capital and more people. The appropriate protection of minority shareholders also played an important role.

Over the years, Corporate Governance has expanded further "down the chain," gradually including in its orbit smaller and private companies but also reaching more specific structures such as family-owned companies and governmental organizations, even while making distinction between international and more locally oriented companies and so on. The reason was obvious: the benefits of Corporate Governance are not really dependent on the size or nature of the company.

An area that has, however, apparently received much less attention is the application of Corporate Governance in startups. This is somewhat in contradiction with the importance given (and rightfully so) to these particular companies: they are an important part of the future backbone for many of the world's economies.

One could obviously ask the question whether such companies require a specific attention or approach when it comes to Corporate Governance. On the basis of a long experience as both Board and coach in startups and as a former CEO of a startup myself, I join other authors in claiming there is a genuine need for such a "specific" approach.

What I also experienced is that Corporate Governance in startups takes or should take a considerably more important role once the company reaches a certain size and becomes a scale-up. Furthermore, the life of a startup does not always follow the path or business plan set forward by the founders-entrepreneurs: in fact, it almost never does and variations are most often not in the positive direction. Therefore it is clear that Corporate Governance should guide the company through the challenges it faces in these growth periods.

No doubt many principles of Corporate Governance apply universally, be it at the level of a startup or a multibillion international group and anything in between. However, as this book will show, the differences from an efficiency point of view are obvious and worth addressing.

A more recent positive development is the attitude of several investors toward startups and their Governance: more than in the past, these investors treat Governance as more than a friendly request before they agree to involve themselves in a company. And the concept definitely comes forward even more prominently when the company moves to a scale-up, which almost always implies raising capital and getting new shareholders on board.

Last but not least, we see a growing interest in complying with ESG criteria (Environment, Social, Governance) both from the general public and from the authorities. This is considerably facilitated through good Corporate Governance from day one. The same applies to CSR (Corporate Social Responsibility). Although today mostly formally limited to bigger companies, the impact of both ESG and CSR on the smallest companies will increase and appropriate governance will be needed for gradual implementation.

Review of earlier publications

Both the amount and quality of publications on Corporate Governance is staggering and growing. From the strictly legal approach to the very practical application, from the family owned companies to the multinationals, from academic research to pure practical training, books and manuals abound.

Three years ago, when I worked on my previous book, there was a big blank in the literature on the specific matter of Corporate Governance in startups.

Today, however, a Google search reveals dozens and dozens of references to studies, books, podcasts, papers, etc. on Corporate Governance in startups. Clearly the world has enthusiastically embraced the concept and benefits of Corporate Governance in this area over the past few years.

The reasons are multiple and well known (and will be repeated in this book). In fact, it is noteworthy that these publications on Corporate Governance particularly in startups originate from very different organizations, ranging from universities, investors, governance associations, etc. and this really on a worldwide scale.

Still, the specific importance and benefits of Corporate Governance in managing the dynamics of a startup in real life practice and in particular the ones making the transition toward a sacle-up are only rarely touched upon.

This book will also highlight this transition governance (which was not covered in my previous book), in the context of discussing the basics of Corporate Governance in our rapidly evolving business environment in general.

My experience

Most of my personal professional experience stems from several years in C-level management positions in larger companies, mostly multinational and international. In the context of being a CEO or managing director of an affiliate in such a larger group, Corporate Governance consists mostly of set of standard operating practices handled largely "on paper" by the legal division, without any significant interference in the day to day management of the subsidiary. Power and responsibilities flow along the lines of hierarchy as set in headquarters. I refer here to an earlier publication on Internal Governance.[2]

Matters are different when you have to work as a CEO with a "real" Board of Directors —an experience I was lucky to have as well. In that case Corporate Governance stands at the center of being able to provide adequate direction and control to the company. I have experienced both the best and the worst in this respect: from the extremely positive impulse a company can get from outstanding governance to the disasters of nonexistent or disruptive Governance potentially bringing the company to fail completely.

In addition to some decades of practical experience in "big" Governance I received formal training in directorship from GUBERNA and the International Directors Program at Insead, which gave me some more insight into the theory of Corporate Governance (including also information on the ongoing research in this area). On the legal front, my years as a lay judge at the court of

2 L. Van den Berghe, L. Sterckx, and H. Ben Salah, *Internal Governance* (Brussels: Intersentia, 2015).

commerce taught me both what the law had to say on Governance and what the dramatic outcomes of noncompliance could be …

All of the above, however, would never have resulted in an ambition to write this booklet on its own. What did inspire me was my second involvement in startups. More than ten years ago I began to get involved with startups, first as an investor (business angel) and coach. Gradually and in fact rather quickly I became more involved in the Board and Governance structures. I quickly appreciated and observed the struggle of these companies to establish an "appropriate" Governance. It took me some time in most of the cases to come to a workable approach, one that was not only possible but also acceptable to all parties involved in Governance. The key was obviously to prove that all these seemingly big and cumbersome efforts would lead to something positive for the company. In one case, I experienced déjà-vu as I also had the pleasure lead-off leading a startup myself (Indaver), which was my first hands-on experience in startups.

Over the past few years, and no doubt amplified by the less favorable economic conditions, startups in which I have been and still am involved in as a Chairman of the Board have faced significant problems—occasionally truly existential. I have become aware that in such circumstances Corporate Governance becomes even more important. The same essentially applies to the transition from startup to scale-up: another moment in which the challenges for a Board and a company are of a completely different nature and importance when compared to "ordinary" business …

2

THE BASICS AND SCOPE

Corporate Governance

The Belgian Code on Corporate Governance defines Corporate Governance as a

> *set of rules and behaviors which determine how companies are managed and controlled.*[3]

The Code further defines Corporate Governance as follows:

> *A good Corporate Governance model will achieve its goal by setting a proper balance between leadership, entrepreneurship and performance on the one hand, and control as well as conformity with this set of rules on the other hand.*
> *Good Governance must be embedded in a company's values. It provides mechanisms to ensure leadership, integrity and transparency in the decision-making process. It should help determine a company's objectives, the means through which these objectives are achieved and how performance is to be*

---

3 https://www.CorporateGovernancecommittee.be/en/about-2009-code/2009-belgian-code-Corporate-Governance; also http://www.codebuysse.com/downloads/CodeBuysseIII_NL.pdf.

evaluated. These objectives should be in the interest of the company, its shareholders and other stakeholders.
Corporate Governance also requires control, i.e. effective evaluation of performance, careful management of potential risks, and proper supervision of conformity through agreed procedures and processes. The emphasis lies on monitoring the effective operation of control systems, managing potential conflicts of interest and implementing sufficient checks to prevent any abuse of power.

Other definitions are similar to this one and occasionally more "mechanical," stressing the importance of mechanisms, decision-making processes, and structures. Furthermore, they sometimes put more emphasis on the relationships between the many different actors/stakeholders in and around the company and explicate the reasons for having Corporate Governance. As such they also represent the beliefs and behaviors that serve as a compass for the company.

It is interesting to observe that the development of Corporate Governance has largely been the result of a number of mishaps in bigger companies. Avoiding reoccurrence of undesirable events is no doubt an initiative meriting praise; yet, however stimulating the positive effects of Corporate Governance are, they have largely remained secondary in its implementation.

The startup company

A startup is defined here as a company that is in the initial stage of its operations.

This implies first of all that we are talking about "a company." Therefore, we consider only organizations/teams that have been structured into some legal company (or association) format. In the context of this book, the startups will be mainly classified as BV/SRL or NV/SA.

Next, the "first stage of operations" above all implies a shortage of just about everything, except probably enthusiasm for a new technology and/or opportunity and a strong motivation "to make it happen." However, at this stage the company likely lacks capital, skills, experience, manpower, structures, procedures, best practices, etc.

It is not easy and maybe also not very useful to put numbers on what defines a startup and to determine the point at which a startup becomes something else.

From a specific Governance viewpoint, it would sometimes appear as if even big companies are still in a startup phase when it comes to professional Corporate Governance ...

For those eager for a concrete definition, one could possibly use the European one for micro-companies: fewer than ten employees and an annual turnover or balance sheet below €2 million, possibly complemented here by a young age and a high growth ambition. The new Belgian Code of Companies and Associations (BCCA) defines (somewhat differently) micro-companies as having a maximum of ten employees, a turnover excluding VAT of maximum 700 k€, and a balance sheet total of maximum 350 k€.

Startups thus differ from SME and large companies in the sense that the dynamics of a startup are mostly different. The startups often reflect a more disruptive and innovative (market) approach and seek to grow quickly, all of which implies a necessity for and a specific approach toward the introduction of Corporate Governance.

For the sake of simplicity, the two key words identifying a startup thus could be "small" and "young."

The scale-up company

There are a number of points where a startup and a scale-up differ.

The first one is obviously time, or more precisely the sequence. Almost by nature, a scale-up follows after a startup, not the reverse. How much later is not really definable, but one can argue that a startup should eventually evolve into a scale-up, at least if it wants to continue on a sustainable growth path. I suggest that this should happen in the range of three to six years after the company is founded, but some slow growers take up to ten years to reach this stage.

So what then defines this step? A number of conditions must be fulfilled. The most important condition is that the product or service should have reached the stage of maturity allowing it to expand without major additional improvements or adaptations. Typically this could be defined as a Technology Readiness Level 9, meaning that the product or idea is fully ready from both a technological and commercial point of view, ready to be produced, and ready to be launched in the targeted market environment.

The next important criterion is growth. The OECD defines a scale-up as a company that has shown growth of turnover and personnel of at least 10–20 percent over the last three years and has more than ten employees. Maybe just as important is the assurance that more growth is indeed possible and likely. One could also refer to the EU definition of the size of (small) companies and claim that a startup is a "micro" company, whereas a scale-up is a "small" company (with personnel exceeding ten people and the turnover or balance sheet total exceeding 2 Mio €). In the remainder of this book, I will use the first definition, as it highlights more strongly the growth dimension.

The final criterion is the increased funding needed to support the growth ambitions. A good reference point seems to be that a scale-up has already received at least 1 Mio € of risk capital over the years. The next round would then most likely imply larger stakes and different, so likely new, shareholders.

Corporate Governance in the startup and scale-up companies

Needless to say, the slow progress of Corporate Governance implementation also applies to the Corporate Governance of startup or scale-up companies. Entrepreneurial founders are generally not extensively trained in or exposed to Governance as they focus on developing a service or a project before anything else.

Additionally, good Corporate Governance takes time to be properly and adequately developed: it is not really a "plug and play" thing. From an implementation point of view, it is therefore wise to consider the time needed for introducing and fully implementing Corporate Governance; the process easily takes three to five years. From that Corporate Governance perspective a startup thus stays a startup during the period of implementation.

The definition of Corporate Governance in a startup or scale-up is not fundamentally different from the one given earlier. This is also neither the place nor the occasion to try to introduce a new definition of Corporate Governance. It is sufficient to readdress the key aspects that apply in particular to a startup. Considering the definition given above, I suggest that the essentials for a startup can be extracted as follows:

> *Corporate Governance is the way the startup is managed and controlled.*
> *Governance establishes a proper balance among different participants in the startup (such as the Board of Directors, managers, and shareholders) and provides the rules for making decisions.*
> *Corporate Governance in a startup is necessary because of the crucial need for leadership through vision and focus and to avoid conflicts of interest between shareholders, founders, and management.*
> *Corporate Governance includes the processes through which strategy and objectives are set and pursued. These include monitoring the company's actions and their impact.*

The attentive reader will have observed that I have eliminated some 70 percent of the wording from the original definition and have added some specific new terms. This in no way means that what has been eliminated is without any significance or value to a startup. It merely highlights the fact that in view of the limited possibilities of a startup one has to extract the essential on which to focus. It should not be forgotten or overlooked that in many cases the perceived complexity of Corporate Governance is seen by startups as the major reason for not giving it too much attention. However, relatively speaking the complexity and diversity of choices and options is frequently broader in a startup than in many bigger companies.

At the same time, given the evolution in size when moving from a startup to a scale-up, Governance does have to adapt. Given the growing complexity, the likely arrival of new investors, the increased complexity, etc., it would seem appropriate to add the following statement to the startup Governance definition:

> *A good Corporate Governance model also ensures control as well as conformity with the set of rules.*
> *It should help determine a company's objectives, the means through which these objectives are achieved, and how performance is to be evaluated.*
> *Corporate Governance also requires control, i.e., effective evaluation of performance, careful management of potential risks, and proper supervision of conformity through agreed procedures and processes.*

Thus, if we compare a startup to a scale-up, the changing environment as a company moves from one stage to the other results inevitably in corporate governance involving a stronger focus on the objectives and more control over how they are reached.

Belgium

Corporate Governance is a pretty universal concept and taught as such all around the world. In reality, however, those implementing it must consider relevant regulations and legislation, which are not quite identical from country to country. This diversity can have a considerable effect on the possibilities and limits for the startup's structuring and operation, as well as on its Board and management forms, statutes, reporting, etc.

For the sake of simplicity, the present booklet confines itself to Belgium. No doubt a significant number of concepts developed further will be valuable and applicable globally, but for the sake of clarity—and in particular with regard to observations related to law—the scope here is Belgium.

BV/SRL and NV/SA

The legal structure of a startup company in Belgium is very frequently a BV (Besloten Vennootschap) / SRL (Société à Responsabilité Limitée) or an NV (Naamloze Vennootschap) / SA (Société Anonyme). Recent relevant legislation in Belgium (Belgian Code of Companies and Associations [BCCA]) still offers a wide variety of company structures (although significantly fewer than under the previous legislation), but the two mentioned above are the most common ones.

In fact, in practice in the past one often saw the evolution of a company from a BV/SRL to an NV/SA in a later stage: originally the company is formed as a BV but at the moment of (substantial) capital increases, it switches into the more "convenient" NV/SA form. It remains to be seen, however, if this practice will continue in the future in Belgium: legislation for companies and associations as of May 1, 2019, may see more BV/SRLs holding on to their initial structure given the broader flexibility given to this form of incorporation than in the past (in particular in relation to a Board of Directors) and the fact that no capital is required. However, the other side of the coin is an increased accountability of the Directors of such companies.

Board of Directors

Referring to the scope of this publication, it is difficult to imagine a realistic minimum quality form of Corporate Governance without a Board of Directors.

The elementary balance in responsibilities and power distribution required in proper Corporate Governance, makes the presence of a real functioning Board of Directors mandatory.

Accordingly, the remainder of this publication assumes that a Board is present and operational. In practice this will come down to discussing the options in an NV/SA (although BV/SRLs could be included as well if they adopt a Board structure as foreseen in the new Belgian Code of Companies and Associations (BCCA)).

3

THE PARTICULARITIES OF A STARTUP / SCALE-UP AND THEIR IMPACT ON GOVERNANCE

What are the key differences between a startup / scale-up and a more mature company from the perspective of Governance?

Typically, when comparing startups or scale-ups to more mature companies, the first element of differentiation to come up is size. Most startups or scale-ups tend to be smaller in size, which can have an effect on the complexity of the company. By that I mean that most of the time a startup or scale-up is more quickly understood than a bigger company (and obviously complexity has an impact on Governance). Size may also influence the issues at stake—again, bigger issues at stake tend to make Governance a more challenging area. This may particularly reflect on the financial amounts at stake, on the return for the shareholders, but equally on the future of employees and other involved stakeholders.

A second element of difference in startups or scale-up when compared to more established and/or bigger companies is lack of experience. One easily overlooks the wealth of experience in bigger companies, including in all aspects of Governance and management, that is most of the time largely absent in a startup or scale-up. These lacking competencies need to be acknowledged when looking at the Governance of startups. When the management is already overwhelmed by the many things to do in a startup environment, this absence of skills and experience is a particular challenge when it comes to Governance. The situation is not improved when the startup or scale-up company is fairly uncomfortable with the use of and reliance upon external specialists. For a scale-up, it sometimes occurs that new investors bring in more experienced board members, but there is no assurance that this will happen ...

Very much linked to this is the absence of data or reference points. Startups are almost always evolving in new fields and areas previously explored vaguely or not at all, be it in technology, products, marketing, approaches, etc. So, in the field of strategy, priority setting or planning in the absence of relevant background information might occasionally be breathtakingly difficult. Certainly for Board members coming from bigger structures, such Governance environments might at first be uncomfortable, to say the least. Again, this situation might be a bit clearer for scale-ups, as their somewhat bigger size should have resulted in the production of more relevant company information.

A third point is the dynamics, the rapid evolution, the impetus toward speedy decisions in startup or scale-up environments. Whether one likes it or not, both startups and scale-ups need to grow quickly and to learn even faster to rapidly adapt the strategy when needed. This comes with a considerable amount of risk taking, more frequently than in bigger companies, which have typically found the right direction of development for their company. Nevertheless these Governance decisions can be and most often are of crucial importance to the further success or failure of the company.

Taking the above into consideration, the Governance in startups or scale-ups does thus differ quite significantly from the Governance of more mature and/or bigger companies in the extent to which risk levels, uncertainties, inexperience, and lack of competencies impact the basis on which Governance is founded. Obviously the absolute impact of decisions (in particular when they are wrong) should be smaller for startups or scale-ups, but that is never really certain, as nobody knows what really lies behind the horizon ... On the other hand, the relative impact could be disastrous and lead to the breakdown of the startup or even the scale-up... Perhaps fragile sums up the particular state of a startup (and to a lesser extent a scale-up).

What are the similarities?

Obviously there are several similarities between the Governance of bigger/more mature companies and that of startups or scale-ups.

First and most obviously, this concerns all legal aspects of Governance. The law makes no or little fundamental distinction (in principle) between the responsibilities of a Board of Directors of a multibillion company versus the board of a startup or scale-up.[4] In all cases, the Board in principal takes on the final responsibilities

4 The 2019 Belgian Code of Companies and Associations (BCCA) established a different maximum liability for Directors depending on the turnover of the company but made no reference to startups. Additionally, there is the specific sphere of listed companies.

(unless defined differently in the articles of association in a situation of dualistic Governance).

However, there are some alternatives here. In the NV/SA situation there is now the option of choosing either a dualistic or a monistic type of Governance (or even a single Director – which is not considered further in this work). The dualistic option makes a distinction between the Board (Raad van Toezicht / Conseil de Surveillance) and the Executive Committee (Directieraad / Conseil de Direction); the monistic type consolidates all Governance in the hands of a Board of Directors (Raad van Bestuur / Conseil d'Administration).

In the case of the BV/SRL, the Governance can be in the hands either of individual Directors or of a group of Directors structured in a Board. All this, however, does not legally differentiate a startup from a bigger-sized company. Of course getting listed on the stock market changes a lot but that is out of the scope of this work.

The second similarity relates to the fundamental duties of the Board of Directors: it sets the strategy, ensures leadership, and holds responsibilities in the area of control. The direction a company is taking obviously includes the views of management and possibly other stakeholders, but it is up to the Board to be the final judge and approve the strategy, including the verification of the rollout plans. Additionally, the Board has the ultimate responsibility with regard to checking if the company operates according to legal and statutory obligations, as well as performing in a satisfactory way in all fields of operation. It is useful here to recall the new accountability of Directors with regard to the liquidity position of a BV/SRL.

The third element is the general responsibility of the Board for the company's adequate operation. This is a vast responsibility but relates primarily and first of all to the right people doing the right things—easily said, not so easily done. The Board should not itself carry out the operational management of the company, but it should ensure the availability of and respect for processes, procedures, standards, and other good operating practices establishing the basis for professional operation. Health and safety, next to environmental respect are key priorities in this field, regardless of the size or age of the company.

Last but not least is the vast field of values and culture. Associated to the vision and mission of the company, values and culture are critical to long-term success and need to be addressed in the context of Corporate Governance. It should be stressed that in the case of a startup the Board has (with the help of management) a unique, not to be missed opportunity and responsibility in the sense that setting a culture at the beginning is much easier than changing or improving it later on. Of particular importance is the attention to safety, not only in respect to avoiding accidents but also in order to generate a culture of care, respect, and professionalism. This closely links also to values such as honesty, transparency, discipline, keeping promises, and commitments: in all of these cases it is obvious that the example should be set at the top, meaning management but also the Board of Directors. It is unrealistic to expect employees to behave in an ethically correct way if the leading figures in the company do not set an example. This equally relates to "simple" things such as the meeting culture: no meeting should be without a purpose, an agenda, a report, an action list with responsibilities, and timing for execution. Starting meetings on time means a lot more than just avoiding people losing time waiting for people who do not show up at the agreed moment: it equally expresses a culture of efficiency and mutual respect.

A strong safety culture has other benefits as well: Environmental respect, cleanliness, attention to health and well-being, etc. all flourish in a strong safety-oriented environment. Incidentally, one should not talk about the "costs" for safety, as it is much more an investment with a considerable return if done well.

Needless to say, such values need to be upheld when moving from a startup to a scale-up.

What is really important in all this?

I guess the conclusion could be that the Governance of a startup or scale-up covers all the essential elements and basic responsibilities of a bigger, more mature company but that in addition to those a startup or scale-up Board has to cope with a number of specific challenges as well as opportunities.

Obviously, the financial or operational impact of Board decisions in terms of € or FTEs and so on is much smaller for startups. Yet, in essence the impact of these decisions is just as, or maybe even more, critical in the sense that a startup usually has a very limited capacity to absorb strategy mistakes.

The two key elements are the fragility of a startup and the need to get it right the first time. Being aware of this helps a startup Board be attentive to the right aspects of Corporate Governance of the company. The "uncertainty factor" is indeed considerable in a startup and inherent in this type of structure and venture.

On the side of the tools to tackle these specific challenges, one has to admit that most of the time startups and scale-ups are less well-equipped to tackle them or to take full advantage of the opportunities at hand. The generally low experience of the management, combined with an occasionally somewhat elementary Board (or no Board at all), are key components of being "underskilled" and do not help in tackling the "uncertainty" factor. But whereas management is most of the time intrinsically connected to the company in that it also comprises the entrepreneurs, this is mostly not the case for the Board of Directors. As will be shown further, this constitutes a basis for bringing in the required experience and skills to the company to get over the "uncertainty" challenge.

In conclusion, one could argue that Corporate Governance should and can make startups and scale-ups go further, faster, and especially with less risk. The latter element is of particular interest given the "uncertainty" factor just referred to.

What makes the difference between Corporate Governance in a startup and a scale-up?

From the above discussion, one would be tempted to think that there are not so many differences between what Corporate Governance should include for a startup versus a scale-up. From a fundamental and legal point of view this is correct. Moreover, there are no explicit rules for changing Corporate Governance when reaching the scale-up stage.

In my view, the change in governance between the startup and scale-up stages should therefore be more considered as a gradual transition to a more professional type of Governance wherein the resources, time, and effort spend on Governance *appropriately* match the needs of the growing company. I cover this point more extensively later in this book. Incidentally, growth should be considered in more than just the financial dimension, more explicitly in the risks implied in the transition. Notably, not only the size but also the nature of the risk tend to evolve from a startup to a scale-up. Whereas in a startup the focus lies (certainly initially) in developing the product, service, or idea into something that is high quality and sellable, in a scale-up the emphasis shifts to the marketing and sale of the same product, service, or idea. Among other changes, this definitely calls for adapted skills and experience in the Board.

In any case, the complexity of Governance grows more than linearly with the size of the company, and Board members should be aware of this. And last but not least: Corporate Governance should be considered a continuous improvement process, meaning for example that in the startup phase improvement steps can and must be taken to address additional challenges.

4

WHAT ARE THE MUST-DO'S?

Legal (company law related) obligations

This is not the place nor the occasion to repeat the vast amount of all applicable legal obligations the startup or scale-up company must follow. However, there are a couple of specific provisions for startups that should be highlighted.

The first one is the obvious need to constitute legally the company in the best possible legal form. There are a number of particular options that are especially important for startup companies. The matter of selecting the company structure is crucial, as it constitutes the future legal backbone of the company's Governance. Obviously, changing the company's legal structure is always possible, but it is time-consuming, burdensome, and expensive. Better thus to do it right the first time. Whether a BV/SRL or an NV/SA or even something else might be the best way to start depends on a lot of factors – as said not the time or place for further details here. The key is to give it proper reflection and collect sufficient insight to make the best choice for the startup, at least for the next two to three years.

Company law stipulates a number of things that need to be agreed among shareholders first and noted down in the company's articles of association. These articles should clearly reflect the purpose of the company. Again the company's future desired development can and should play a role in what is registered here. Governance of the company and particular shareholder rights will probably get the highest attention.

Once the company is constituted, quite an impressive slew of legal obligations will have to be respected, whether it is a small startup company or not. Obviously this is a priority for any company, including a startup, but this does not imply the company has to complete the process all by itself. Still, selecting the right help is not always obvious—in my experience, the occasional selection of the accountant, lawyer, etc. from among "old friends from around the corner" quickly proves not to have the broad enough shoulders to adequately serve the startup, once it comes to somewhat more complicated legal areas. I therefore recommend starting from the beginning with a high enough competence level of service to provide the company with (especially) the required accounting and reporting. No surprise that this becomes even more obvious when transitioning to the stage of a scale-up ...

Representation of the company to the outside world is also a matter with a legal dimension that should be addressed. Normally this is up to the CEO but it is good practice to install the four-eyes principle, meaning two people signing off. These rules can be registered in a DOA (delegation of authority) or similar document to be approved by the Board of Directors. Such a DOA should be one of the business processes to be formalized in the course of time. To be opposable to third parties, such a DOA needs to be published in the *Belgian Official Gazette*.

Last but not least: both from a perspective of quality and efficiency I recommend turning to professional advice and services for finalizing most of the above ...

When things turn ugly ...

It is a legal requirement to have, among other things, a financial plan when registering a new company (note: such a financial plan should help the founders identify the required starting capital; there is a specific founders' liability applicable in case of bankruptcy within three years). However, reality will never completely match the figures listed in such plans, no matter how carefully they have been prepared. On top of that, more often than not, reality is (considerably) worse than anticipated. Most of the time this has a negative impact on the financial position of the company. Board members in those circumstances should be very aware of the obligation as stated in the Code of Companies and Associations (BCCA) to look at the continuity of the company over the next twelve months on a regular basis, as well the obligation to sound the alarm bell procedure when required (when the net assets to the equity division is below 50 percent or 25 percent). This latter step involves the calling of a shareholders' meeting by the Board (procedures vary somewhat between an NV/SA and a BV/SPRL; for a BV/SPRL, an additional limit is when the equity goes below the minimal equity level or becomes negative for a BV/SPRL). Nota bene: the company's articles of association may stipulate an even more stringent set of rules for the circumstances triggering the alarm bell procedure.

In practice, I have found these obligations a bit strange when it comes to starting companies, as one would assume that such companies are focused on investing their capital into their development and thus almost unavoidably "eat up" their capital while not yet able to generate sufficient profits. Still, the above-mentioned regulations are included in the Belgian Code of Companies and Associations (BCCA) and failing to respect them might entail the personal liability and accountability of Board members.

An even more dramatic situation can occur when the company runs out of funds, still has sufficient sales but is experiencing a substantial cash burn, and has difficulties getting loans/credits or additional capital. In those circumstances, book XX of the Economic Law Code applies. Next to defining the conditions under which a company has to declare bankruptcy (essentially failing to pay outstanding invoices plus being unable to get new credit) it also covers among many other points the case known as "wrongful trading." This relates to the situation where a company continued operation where it should have known that it had no future. Again, this could imply personal liability for the Board members, but as before I would not endeavor to cover this more comprehensibly as it is a specific and complicated matter better left to more competent people.

In conclusion: when the company gets in dire straits, beware of the particular responsibilities you have as a Board, ... and get a good lawyer involved.

Shareholders agreement

Obviously, for shareholders to agree upon and regulate their future cooperation, more is needed than just the articles of association. A considerable amount of detail and attention is often given to the procedures for changing shareholding or increasing capital, as well as to the representation of different individuals and groups in the decision structures such as the Board of Directors, the committees (if any), and the management. Other ways of avoiding conflict include reporting content and frequency. While it is good to think about all this, one has equally to consider that a startup's circumstances tend to evolve both quickly and unexpectedly. Accordingly, shareholder agreements should provide the required flexibility and speed to resolve these challenges without going through procedures that are too elaborate and time-consuming.

A particular subgroup of shareholders are the entrepreneurs/founders. The matter is quite simple if there is only one entrepreneur/founder, but most of the time there are two or even three or more. Although it is frequently overlooked as not being important or relevant, I would strongly advocate an agreement within this group. That agreement should specifically stipulate how a situation where one of the entrepreneurs departs should be handled—including the financial aspects in full detail and with a limited amount of ad hoc interpretation. Additionally, such an agreement should preferably cover the individual professional contribution of each founder and establish conditions for exiting (or transferring to a new entrant if required).

Unfortunately, whereas entrepreneurs/founders start as friends and good colleagues, things can turn sour in the following years, not to speak of more dramatic exits caused by serious disease or even loss of life. In those cases it is significantly helpful to resolve the situation as quickly as possible and thus give the company the best chance to continue and survive. That is why such agreements should be made, and the earlier it is done, the better.

Codes, rules, and regulations

Let's start here by making a clear distinction between what is, on the one hand, an obligation foreseen in official regulations or legislation and all other constraints, on the other (so called soft-law).

As far as obligations are concerned, the answer is very simple: there is no excuse whatsoever for not respecting applicable obligations set in the law or in official regulation. Ignorance of the law excuses no one ... Unfortunately, sometimes one observes the "small size" of a company being used as an excuse for bypassing or neglecting some of these. This is both foolish and inefficient: foolish because this simply does not constitute a valid argument for not respecting the obligation, and inefficient because one will have to comply eventually, most likely at a higher cost and possibly with an additionally imposed penalty. "Do it right the first time" gets all its meaning here. Particular points of interest include regulations within the context of social law, tax law, company law, environmental and safety legislation, specific compliance, etc.

If addressing the other soft-law area of codes, rules, and recommendations that are not absolutely mandatory, the matter can be approached in a more relaxed way. That being said, it remains important to keep an open mind toward these as they are mostly merely a reflection on "how to do things better" based on the experiences and mistakes of other companies. Also before court, "soft"-law occasionally shows some very "hard" sides ... Some may also be mandatory, or at least very much appreciated (if not demanded) by customers, such as quality certification (ISO 9000 and related) or safety certification (such as VGA). Within this framework one could also consider a Code of Conduct or similar document reflecting the beliefs and expected behaviors of all involved in or around the company. The vastness of these excludes a detailed discussion, but in the framework of Corporate Governance there are a couple of further interesting items that will be addressed later in this booklet.

Last but not least: everything stated in this section increases in importance when moving into a scale-up.

Publications and reporting

I am treating this as a separate point because in the heat of the battle of a startup I have regularly observed that this is overlooked. Being part of the legal obligations, publications and reporting are frequently not well known to the management (and sometimes to the Board) but can be of significant importance to the Governance bodies and their accountability. I am in particular thinking of the so-called alarm bell procedure (see also above), but also Board composition (changes), annual shareholders meeting, the UBO (Ultimate Beneficial Owner), certain specific statutory or shareholder agreement reporting obligations, DOA (Delegation of Authority), and so forth. Timely and complete fulfillment of the reporting obligations is in fact a no brainer, but that is more easily and quickly said than done ... It should not be forgotten that the absence of proper publication can make decisions void and ineffectual. Additionally, it can involve Director liability ... Nota bene: publication makes board decisions objectionable to third parties and should therefore be the general rule, but board decisions always remain valid inside the organization, whether they are published or not.

When reaching the scale-up level all this does become necessary rather than merely desirable. If sometimes irregular, late, or imprecise reporting can be the case in (early) startups, in the scale-up phase it is no longer permissible. With the increasing risks, the Governance should be based of precise, timely, and concise data. Most of the time, the scale-up phase also involves a different type of investors, for whom sloppy communication is an unacceptable alternative.

5

CHOICES IN CORPORATE GOVERNANCE

Company structure

The new Belgian Code of Companies and Associations (BCCA) has somewhat simplified and considerably reduced the possible legal structures for a company, startup, or other venture. The formerly preferred structure for a startup was the BVBA/SPRL, essentially because of its simplicity and lower capital need. This structure has now been replaced with the BV/SRL, and the new company law overcomes a number of the inflexibilities that characterized the former BVBA/SPRL: rights given to shares can vary substantially and the Governance structure can be adapted to the growth of the company. A BV/SRL can even be listed on the stock market. Given these adaptations, it remains to be seen if the "usual" transition from a BVBA/SPRL to an NV/SA will still involve the traditional step-up in such cases, as a substantial enlargement of shareholding, merger, or acquisition.

From that perspective, the changes to the former NV/SA structure are less pronounced and could be summarized as giving more options and flexibility to the company. Most likely the NV/SA structure will remain the most popular one for bigger and stock market– listed companies. Additionally, the increased Director's accountability in a BV/SRL with regard to the company's financial resources might stimulate transition to an NV/SA.

Both NV/SA and BV/SRL now have the possibility to limit their Board/Governance structure to just one Director. From a Governance point of view it is doubtful whether this constitutes progress ...

For the sake of completeness: the other remaining company structures are not covered here.

Why (immediately) a BOD?

Occasionally startups do not fully exploit the possibilities of a "real" BOD (although it is a formal legal requirement) but prefer to start with a board of advisors. Starting with such an advisory board will, however, at best remove some emotional hurdles of bringing in "strangers" to the company and show that these "strangers" can indeed bring new and valuable things to the company. These types of advisory Boards essentially just postpone the needed injection of real, high-quality and professional Governance to the startup. The most important aspect here is, in my opinion, the checks and balances brought in by professional Board members.

Obviously a "real" BOD is not a matter of choice anymore when reaching the scale-up level. An even more properly composed, professional, and experienced BOD is then a must. The above does not exclude the possibility and potential value of an advisory Board, supporting management and / or the Board of Directors in a particular field (usually for a specified time with a concrete target).

BOD composition ... and the Chair

Like it or not: startup, scale-up, or other category, if you incorporate a company structure, then a formal Governance structure is a legal must, be it that the Governance structure can be limited to just one person/company. From a good Governance perspective this is not the recommended setup— lone wolves are not the examples I would like to refer to in the context of adequate Governance, be it in startups or more mature companies.

Let's try to approach the crucial question of Board composition from a set of concrete principles (as I've said, a BOD is the preferred Governance structure).

First principle: the primacy of the shareholders

The Board of Directors is always appointed by the shareholders. The Board should make sure that the company accomplishes the statutory goals and objectives set by the shareholders in the Articles of Association. The Directors are required to justify this Governance to the shareholders.

Second principle: quality and competence are important, not power

It remains remarkable, although understandable, that so many Board compositions are set up so as to "reflect the shareholders' positions" in the company. This concept does not always fit well with the best Governance of the company, nor with the legal obligation of a Director to put the interest of the company before the interest of the shareholder. In fact the law does only recognize a Director of a Board of a company, not a Director "of a particular shareholder of that same company." Insisting on a formal representation of shareholders in a Board of Directors does or can have a positive motivation in making sure the company gets adequate high-quality and committed support; however, the underlying reason also frequently originates from a lack of trust and an urge to influence the company in a direction most appropriate for a particular shareholder, when needed. Well-intended as it may be, it remains suboptimal, to say the least. Also being adequately informed on what goes on in the company is often given as a reason for direct shareholder representation. But avoiding having "passengers" on the Board is important. Negligence is a cause of liability for any individual Director.

Finally it should not be overlooked that the quality and competence of the Board members should encompass the interests of all the stakeholders: a company operates in a much broader context than just management and shareholders.

Third principle: complementary and synergy with management prevail over power and control

A startup is by my definition a structure with limited resources, people, and means— including Governance and management. So even more than in other companies, double work and overcontrol should be avoided at all cost. The spirit of the Directors should be one of complementarity with management: most of the company management are (young) entrepreneurs with generally a limited experience in both Governance and management. Developing, coaching, and even teaching of management should be considered as an important task and responsibility.

The above obviously does not free the Board of Directors of their end-of-the-line responsibilities in terms of strategy setting and control. But a good Board gives a CEO and his/her team wings ...

Fourth principle: the Chairman is crucial

No doubt Chairing a Board is a particular task, be it a startup or not. As the "primus inter pares," the Chair "manages" the Board, but in the context of a startup or scale-up the role also includes even more direct contact, via coaching and mentoring the CEO. The bridging function between CEO and Board is one of particular importance in general, but even more particularly in startups. In the context where one has a generally less experienced, entrepreneurial, and very dynamic CEO this requires specific diplomatic and other skills. But it doesn't stop there, as the Chair should also function as the key contact for shareholders, be it the entrepreneurs or the external capital providers. And last but not least: there are other stakeholders to whom a company in general and the Board in particular should pay attention, and here the Chair plays the role of making sure they are adequately involved and informed.

The Chair needs to maintain the balance between the three actors comprising the governance tripod: shareholders, executives, and the Board. For that reason, the Chair must manage different points of view adequately during the Board meetings.

In my experience, all of this works best or has at least a higher chance of success in a case where the Chairman is an independent Director. This will give him or her the kind of intellectual freedom to consider the different interests and stakeholder groups.

Needless to say the combination of CEO and Chair in the same person implies serious risks in terms of keeping the right checks and balances. It also risks the Board operating in a pretty sterile atmosphere.

So what should the Board composition look like?

First of all, to keep things workable, the size of the Board should be limited. Next to possibly one or two entrepreneurs-founders-CEO-managers who serve as executive Directors, three to four additional nonexecutive Directors should do the job, thus giving you a total of four to six people. That concept should not change when moving to the scale-up level.

Secondly, in order to keep things in balance, the presence of independent Directors is highly recommended. In particular this concerns the Chair, given the large spread of points of attention the Chair has to monitor and stimulate appropriately, meaning taking into account the interests of all stakeholders of the company. Additionally, it is recommended that the Board includes more than one independent Director, especially when facing regular risks of conflicts of interest involving other Board members (see further)

Thirdly, real quality comes with diversity: nothing is as sterile as a Board composed of clones. Gender diversity is a positive target but should be second to the competence of the individual candidate. And obviously (extreme) diversity could lead to incomprehensibility ... There has to be a common understanding of and support for what the company is aiming to achieve. Diversity should by the way not be limited to gender, as it sometimes is, but should encompass education, age, background, culture, etc. if possible.

Fourthly, the Board composition should be such that at least the following basic competencies are available in the Board:

- profound understanding of and if possible hands-on experience in a startup
- insight into the business of the startup, in particular its commercial aspects
- knowledge of Corporate Governance principles and practice
- strategy development and follow-up
- human capital development
- general CEO/management skills (in particular useful for the Chair)
- finance and legal

The Board should have the different competencies to handle the variety of challenges the company will face. In particular, this includes good knowledge of the needs of the business of customers the company intends to reach.

Obviously, having two identical profiles in the Board doesn't really help from an efficiency point of view. The table in addendum 1 may be of help in setting up Board member profiles in the case of setting up a new Board or when replacing one of the Board members. Another point to remember is that unfortunately the Board often has to compensate for the lack of experience at the level of the managers-entrepreneurs …

Fifthly, there are values that every Board member should exhibit, support, and propagate: ethics, honesty, integrity, transparency, fairness, and team spirit. Judgment skills, authenticity, and maturity also help. On an individual level Directors must be willing and able to work hard and put in the necessary time, even at unplanned moments. As I've said: no passengers … A last prerequisite: some patience helps in a startup Board …

The board has to function as a collegial body, where high quality decisions are preferably reached by consensus. This concerns the issue of having sound board dynamics. The debate during the meeting should be constructive. Differences of opinion and alternative approaches should be welcomed. Directors should challenge each other's opinions, without letting the debate overheat or letting it be dominated by one individual or a clique within the board. Needless to say, the Chair plays an important role here ...

Having said all this, it is quite possible that this "optimal" approach is not really realistic in startups, at least not from day one. There are two major obstacles. The first is the usual course of events in a startup where (young) entrepreneurs have developed a concept, idea, product, or service and are eager to start a company developing it into a real business. Although they usually do not fit the above-mentioned principles or Director profile needs, they will very rarely accept not being on the Board once the company is launched. The second obstacle is usually the external funding parties, be they business angels, Corporate ventures, private investors, or government agencies: they are virtually always more than interested in being on the Board of Directors, to put it mildly.

Obviously all these groups will bring their great motivation and commitment to the success of the startup. There are, however, two caveats. The first is that their interests might not really be 100 percent identical to those of the company, and the second that there are no doubt elements of power distribution involved. These challenges need to be clearly understood and monitored. Overcoming them can be at least partially attempted through application of the above-mentioned principles/guidelines, as well as through referring to the legal obligation that Directors only and uniquely serve the interest of the company on which Board they are. So if external investors demand representation on the Board, they should be invited to provide profiles best fitting the need of the Board of the company. A professional selection process always pays off in these cases … More easily said than done, I must admit.

Allow me also to address the shareholder representative as Director on the Board with a particular interest in developing (commercial or other) synergies with the company. Often this is introduced in a very positive way—like "together our two companies can accomplish miracles" or "this is really going to be a win-win for both" and so forth. And in cases I have witnessed things indeed start rather optimistically, until it becomes clear that there is an obvious imbalance in information and interests. Ultimately, a euro cannot be in two pockets at the same time …, it is a simple as that. The required exclusion of such a board member when matters such as production costs, marketing margin, and so on are discussed in order to maintain corporate governance leads regularly to clashes in the Board, which could have been avoided if from day one it would have been understood that the better way would have been a simple (be it privileged or special) commercial agreement rather than a capital investment and a Board mandate …

A word also on "Observers" in the Board of Directors. When it comes to some Committees (see further), these seats are more often than not a question of making sure that all shareholders get (in their view) a balanced and proper representation in the governance structures of the company. Needless to say, it is more than likely a compromise in order to avoid having "too many board members." Formally, an observer is an individual with the right to attend and participate in Board meetings, the same as any other director. The observers receive any information the ordinary directors receive before meetings, too. Obviously these individuals do not have the same voting rights as other directors. Usually, they are or represent people who have a significant stake in the company.

Meeting agenda, structure, and frequency – what should the BOD really do?

Given the limited resources of a startup (also of a scale-up) and the vast amount of things to do at hand, efficiency of Governance in general and of the Board's meeting in particular is thus of the greatest importance. A small company's success is not dependent on the amount of reporting and quantity of papers to the Board. A judicious choice of the points to be handled at the Board meetings is therefore really crucial.

The first danger for a Board to look out for is not shifting rapidly in a short-term oriented, semi-operational, almost managerial, ad hoc type of agenda. Such an agenda will deal with the no doubt numerous and frequently unforeseen and urgent points of (possible) attention popping up in the highly dynamic and unpredictable environment of many startups. No doubt the house might sometimes seem (or actually is) "on fire"— in which case, all should help to extinguish the fire, if there is one. But the Board should absolutely avoid continuous firefighting mode. When this happens, action needs to be taken because operating in such a way risks doubling up work that management should be doing. Furthermore, it brings substantial risks in terms of the Board not addressing the long-term challenges it should be focused on. A way to at least partially overcome this is to set an agenda to which the Board sticks at each meeting. A good quote I picked up referring to this "detail-active interfering Board" is: "*The board should stick its head in the tent, but its hands should stay outside the tent.*"

In essence, each meeting addresses the ad hoc situation of the company (typically HSEQ, finance, commercial, operational), followed by a longer session addressing one or two particular, longer-term subjects for the company such as strategy, annual plan and budget, human capital, marketing and sales, financial structure, etc. It is recommended to set up such a plan for the whole year (an example is given in Addendum 2). The Board should be able to "look over the hill," meaning it should consider not just present-day and imminent issues but also those further ahead in time. Risks are indeed high that management will not have the time (nor sometimes the skills) to come to such reflections early enough, leaving the company without a really accurate and effective compass. "Focus" being one of the most important priorities for a startup as well as a scale-up, one can hardly understand that this "focus" can be effectively and efficiently implemented without a set strategy direction. Working in such a way will allow the company not only to extinguish the fires but also to discuss measures on how to prevent reoccurrence.

Structuring the meeting is important in several ways, and the interaction of the CEO with the Chair is key to this structuring. There are a couple of takeaways here. In order to avoid wasting time on items that should not or cannot benefit from Board discussions, it is worthwhile to make clear which items are for information only and which ones demand decision. Linked to this, it is important that appropriate documentation is sent beforehand (three working days in advance should be considered a minimum) to the Board; needless to say, here the quality is more important than the quantity. The information received should in principle be sufficient to make evidence-based decisions and relate to the overall strategy and not delve too deep into operational details.

Nota bene: directors need to respect confidentiality rules with regards to the information received, the debate during the board, and the conclusions reached as reflected in the meeting minutes.

The frequency of the Board meetings is defined by the needs of the company but also conditioned by the resources available. I realize this says everything and nothing at the same time. In reality, the situation is always different and it is hardly possible to predict what a "good" meeting frequency might look like for a particular company. However, we can definitely speak of a minimum frequency, as the law mandates the Board's decision on certain items (annual results, agenda shareholders' meeting, etc.). Within the same legal framework, a number of provisions definitely demand an engagement of the Board, which is best not just performed "on paper." To clarify, I would like to repeat that I do not consider the "lone wolf" one (wo) man Governance structure really appropriate for those challenges.

On the other hand, startup companies have limited resources and can hardly be asked to produce, let's say, a detailed pack of relevant documents for conducting a quality Board meeting on a monthly basis. As I said before, the contribution of a Board is determined not by the quantity but by the quality of the information at hand. This is generally true for any Board, but in the particular situation of a startup the limited resources from the side of management take a specific importance.

On balance, in my experience, a frequency of five meetings per year would be advisable in a "steady" environment, four being an absolute minimum and six maybe a bit "luxurious." As given in Addendum 2, the subjects that should be addressed by a "normal" Board mandate and justify four meetings.

Of course, these recommendations only cover "normal" Board meetings. In practice it is almost unavoidable to have more meetings, in particular in relation to problems and themes occurring outside the "regular" Board agenda and context. Examples may include sudden departures of key people, cash emergencies, sudden investment opportunities, etc. A particular point of interest here is the previously mentioned so-called Alarm Bell Procedure which in the new BCCA (Belgian Code of Companies and Associations) now not only implies virtual continuous monitoring of the net assets of the company but also includes a regular reflection on the company's future evolution.

Committees

Board committees (such as Audit, Remuneration, Strategy, Nomination, etc. Committees) in startups are more the exception than the rule. Only very rarely will a formal Board committee be needed or justified. Another matter is an advisory committee, which is not composed of Board members but rather of outside specialists advising the Board and management on specific issues. Frequently their activities revolve around technical and scientific aspects of the business, where particular high level expertise is requested. Their contribution could also relate to market introduction of products and services or pricing issues. As is understood in the wording, an advisory committee cannot be held accountable for its recommendations: the Board will hold final decision and responsibility.

Finally, a little caveat for advisory committees created for "keeping all shareholders satisfied," meaning everybody gets a little role in the company. Such—possibly unintentional—objectives blur the only justifiable reason for an advisory committee, which is accessing expertise that is not available in the company structures. As we know, representation and competence are not necessarily identical ...

With regard to the transition to scale-up, one often observes the desire to create a Remuneration Committee. The challenge of compensating management in line with the strategic objectives and plans of the company becomes more important and linked to the sensitivity of the subject. As such, a specific Committee is seen as the appropriate way to discuss these matters and prepare advice for the Board. As far as the composition of such a committee is concerned, it is usually limited to three members, including the Chairman of the Board and obviously excluding conflicted Board members (which are usually the founders/managers).

Relationship investors - BOD - management

In most startups, the triad of shareholders - Board of Directors - management exhibits some particularities.

First, the entrepreneurs/founders at the origin of many a startup are usually shareholder, Director and manager all in one. As we know that these three roles are different from a Governance perspective, it is not obvious to resolve the problem that one person can hardly adequately play three roles at the same time. Still, there is no obvious solution to this problem.

Second, because much of the time the startup needs external funding, a specific group of shareholders—"the investors"—is equally specific. If they do not belong to the FFF category,[5] they will be actively and rightfully interested in how the company evolves.

5 FFF = friends, family, and fools.

Third, the fact that shareholders are represented to a considerable extent on the Board makes information of these shareholders a nonissue.

When moving to the scale-up level, these relationships become different and even more complex in some aspects. One reason is that the number of shareholders is likely growing, and not all of them will be given an individual seat on the Board. Additionally, the impact and authority of the founders usually diminishes over time and some might have to leave the management and / or the Board.

Such changes move the relationships into a more formal process, in which a more strict adherence to communication and decision-making is required. To put it differently: this is when management, the Board, and shareholders move to their formal role and responsibilities as given in "normal" circumstances in a more mature company. In these circumstances, it is useful to indicate responsibility in the area of communication to the shareholders (see for example the Charter of the Board of Directors in Appendix 5).

Evolution and evaluation

Regardless of these particularities, Governance in startups and scale-ups will depend as in any company on the respect for the specific role each group has to play: shareholders own the company and eventually decide on its future, the Board holds (by appointment by the shareholders) the key responsibility for the company, and management (by delegation of the Board) executes and follows through daily operations. It is fundamental that each group respects these roles and allows for the checks and balances necessary to effectively execute their tasks. A too clubby atmosphere should be avoided: when difficult points have to be addressed, they should be brought to the table. When transitioning to a scale-up, this becomes even more necessary.

Regular pitfalls or at least suboptimal situations involve (external) shareholders getting involved in detailed Board activities (without actually belonging to the Board) or even into daily operations; Board members or even shareholders taking over from management in selecting lower level personnel or suppliers, etc. These kind of behaviors are detrimental to the quality, efficiency, and effectiveness of the company, and thus improvement of the different Governance levels is mandatory in such cases. As we all know, it is quite difficult to be a good judge of oneself, even when considering the fact that authority and power come with responsibilities. Mixing management, Board and shareholders too much or neglecting the necessity to make a clear distinction between the three is thus to be avoided. Operating "at arm's length" is the right attitude. If not applied, the risks of conflict of interests frequently abound ...

Again, in practice this is easier said than done. A key role here is the one to be played by the Chairman of the Board: he or she should be the guardian of the essential separation of tasks and responsibilities, even in the not-so-obvious context of having the same people on the different levels. The key thing is to ensure everyone is reminded of their particular role and responsibility when a specific topic is discussed.

A couple of examples might make this clear. Discussion of a capital increase (NV/SA) or contribution (BV/SRL) takes another tone and interest when conducted by the Board of Directors compared to the shareholder level. Preparing the annual accounts as management needs to do is not the same as clearing them for submission to shareholders' approval, as the Board should do. Conflict of interest situations, which are natural in startups with the same people on different levels, mandate very clear and transparent handling: this can only be done by making clear at what level the discussion is to be taken and to follow the process through in making sure it is done at the appropriate level. When it comes to nominating people, the good practice is for the Board to approve managers reporting directly to the CEO (members of the management committee) but to leave all other nominations entirely up to that management, as long as they stay within the agreed budgets and plans.

The implementation of good Corporate Governance in a startup is mostly a matter of learning and improving along the way. In the often-hectic environment of getting a company launched, Governance seldom gets the priority it deserves (although this appears to be changing). Anyway, at the start the situation will be what it is, which is probably a long distance away from "best" Governance practices. That should not necessarily be too negative, provided there is consensus on continuous improvement of the Governance process. Again, the Chair should take a leading role in advancing this goal. Obviously, the process starts with an implicit or explicit review of points to be improved, where as usual those points that are likely to see a substantial improvement for a limited effort should be discussed first. Being fairly minimalistic at the start, this evolution should involve some form of evaluation of the functioning of Governance in general and of the Board in particular. Again, this is easier said than done, given also the regular personal sensitivities related to evaluations. Needless to say, such processes must be introduced step by step, in full transparency, specifically when it comes to the objectives and with respect to privacy and individual attitudes.

It is clear that the Board has a duty to continuously improve its functioning. A startup should not and cannot make an exception to this rule. However, as I have already said, the evaluation exercise needed in this process should be gradually implemented (starting, for example, with a simple verbal evaluation of the meeting's quality at the end of it). It can be extended afterward by launching individual talks between the Chair and the individual Directors. Obviously the summary should be reported and actions should be taken for improvement. Once more the role of the Chair is crucial in this delicate process ...

One last point regarding the relationship between Board and management. It sometimes happens that management—especially when it is largely the founders/entrepreneurs—has significant issues with Board meetings. Being focused 100 percent on "making their business work," they do not always understand why so much time and effort need to be spent on these Board meetings, which, if they are not efficiently run, may seem a waste of time. This is again a crucial point of attention for the Chairman. No matter how legally required these meetings are, the motivation of management to join the Board process and proceedings is crucial. When exiting the Board meeting, the management should feel more motivated and exited than when entering that same meeting. When that can be given as a conclusion after a board meeting, the relationship is where it should be. It is about working together in a Board, rather than working against each other.

Remuneration

The question of whether startup Board members should be remunerated is a relevant one and occasionally very debated, carrying a high level of sensitivity. By definition, financial resources in a startup are limited, which is often cited as an argument for not paying Directors and certainly not Directors who are also shareholders (as "they are working for their own money") or managers/founders (as "they are already paid as a manager" and "will get a big upside"). Despite the "logic" of these arguments, it is clear that they do not respond to the separate tasks and responsibilities of the Board of Directors. The opinion that Directors need to be professionals and accordingly compensated for their work is very broadly accepted in codes of Governance which make no distinction between startups and bigger companies (even though a reality-based distinction is often made between external Directors and those who are either shareholders or managers).

Suppliers will not provide a startup with the services and products it requires for free, just because it is a smaller-sized startup. It is difficult to see that this should be different for Board Directors. In current recommendations,[6] the Director's remunerations consider the (often) rather limited complexity of the startup or scale-up as well as the lower (financial) risks associated, which results in lower packages.

---

6 GUBERNA 2012 publication "Vergoeding voor externe bestuurders van een kmo" – https://www.guberna.be/nl/know/guberna-hoe-moeten-start-ups-en-scale-ups-hun-bestuurders-vergoeden.

Reality is today not always aligned with these recommendations. Contemporary practice still favors zero compensation for shareholder-Directors and for entrepreneur-manager-Directors, while allowing (small) remunerations for independent external Directors but even in these cases zero compensation still occurs, making it a kind of voluntary work. A small compensation for external Directors being better than nothing, I would still advocate a remuneration for all Board members, certainly in those cases where not all shareholders are Directors or not all entrepreneurs are Directors. A Directorship if done well—is a considerable and specific task and responsibility, requiring the right experience and training and cannot be treated as a purely voluntary contribution (and certainly not in the longer run).

Last but not least, the remuneration for the Chair should be substantially higher than for other Directors given both the higher responsibly and greater workload. Typically a double (or triple) level of remuneration is practiced. A practical table is in Addendum 7.

Nota bene: the BCCA (Belgian Code of Companies and Associations) now stipulates (both for NV/SA and BV/SRL) that Directors are to be remunerated, unless specified differently in the Articles of Association or in a specific decision taken by the General Meeting of Shareholders ...

Another question that should be addressed is whether the remuneration should be a fixed one (not taking into account the number of Board meetings or other itemized work), a variable one (most likely a particular sum per Board meeting and/or a payment for separate work on, for instance, an hourly basis) or a combination of the fixed and variable options. Many companies apply a mixed system (as recommended by GUBERNA—see previous reference). It is, however, worthwhile to reflect on the underlying principles of the remuneration practices selected by the Board. A variable or mixed system often assumes that having more meetings implies more hours worked and thus mandates a higher sum to be paid. On the other side, a Directorship may be considered a general responsibility and the implication of a Director should be complete, no matter how many hours this takes. My recommendation would be to select a fixed remuneration per month, which should represent a financial compensation for all the work done, be it more or be it less.

A last word on the compensation package for the founders who are also directors and (possibly large) shareholders. When incorporating a company for the first time, this question of remuneration is probably not in the foreground of the concerns of these entrepreneurs. However, the matter inevitably pops up when external investors join the capital of the startup. It is then not uncommon to agree on a (very) low compensation for these founders, considering the important upside they could have on their capital share, which then additionally also can be mixed in a convenient valuation of the startup. This kind of understanding could then hold for some time, but a number of clouds usually appear on the horizon when reaching the scale-up phase.

At that moment the "big upside" might not be so "big" anymore, and possibly or certainly not as quick as hoped for; less wealthy founders might be confronted with some scarcity of personal financial resources and new shareholders might not be willing to join the initial high company valuation. … The result: a highly sensitive discussion on the compensation package of what is possibly the most important human resources asset of the company: its top management. … I must stress here that no situation is identical and various possibly gradual solutions can be worked out for in these cases. What I have seen, however, is that in the end, whether convenient or not, the ultimate solution lies in coming to a compensation package in line with the market practices for the function (CEO, CTO, etc.). That remuneration should include the individual's responsibility as an executive director where applicable. As a shareholder, they would additionally benefit like any of the shareholders. Only by clearly separating the different roles / responsibilities and compensating individuals on their own merits can one achieve a quantifiable and justifiable basis for resolving these questions in the longer run. The twin side of this approach is that each of the founder-managers should also understand that their performance in a particular function should fully match the requirements of that function. If not, a replacement can and should be executed.

Continuity

It should be noted that both the Board and the company should benefit from some minimal continuity and consistency in the composition of the Board. There are several aspects here. First of all, Directors need time to fully master and comprehend the specifics of a startup and later a scale-up. While a business plan may provide the startup's expected environment, strategy, and outcome, the reality is often quite displeasingly different. And here comes the second point: the importance of learning why it is different and what can successfully be done to correct the situation if necessary. That learning process is important for drafting and approving the future direction of the company. Last but not least: the Board should work as a team and it is hard to imagine how this can be achieved with a Board whose composition changes significantly every year or so. In this respect, the occasional practice of appointing a Director for the first year or so to oversee that things get off to a good start and replacing him or her after that period is not really optimal.

Incidentally, it is good practice to have the Board meeting also occasionally informally over dinner: a teambuilding exercise can be that simple.

To close this reflection on continuity: after a longer period of time (say five to six years), the situation is different and in those circumstances a replacement plan should be set up to gradually bring in fresh Directors to avoid tunnel vision and introduce new ideas. This should be planned well ahead of time in order not to face a situation where too many Directors leave at the same moment, taking away the memory bank of the Board ... In moving to a scale-up, the arrival of new shareholders obviously can also be seen as a way to bring in new competencies, often required given the new environment the company will be entering.

6

THE TRANSITION FROM STARTUP TO SCALE-UP

The awakening

The ceremony of the incorporation of the startup being concluded before the notary, the startup embarks enthusiastically on its mission: turning the dream of the founders into reality. Indeed a lot of drive, motivation, and enthusiasm will be needed, as this is never an easy process.

After getting a lot of practical things organized (needed but time consuming ...), it is then time to sharpen the concept of a product or service into something marketable. Most frequently this takes more time than planned or expected. What the founders had in mind most often doesn't fit precisely with the wishes of the future customers or just exhibits essential flaws that need correction. One extreme example I came across was that the service was much too limited in application scope to have any significant sales potential. As a consequence, the company had to completely redesign its original ambition, technology, and business plans. Obviously, this takes time. Another frequently encountered phenomenon is where founders-engineers endlessly continue the development of their product. Aiming for perfection is certainly not negative, but in the context of a startup this comes into conflict with the by-definition limited funds (and limited patience of the investors). Again, from personal experience, this leads to the removal of founders / managers in order to reorient the company into a satisfactory product design, ready for full-scale production and marketing.

Meanwhile, attempts are made to sell whatever the startup has for sale. However—and this is linked in my eyes to the "developer" nature of most founders—there is often too little structure and even less priority given to this marketing and sales process.

Often this attitude (which is obviously not the right one if the company is to be sustainable) is extended through subsidies. Certainly they are welcomed and beneficial but often do not really help make the founders realize that in the end the company needs successful and growing sales to survive. One would say that they do not really create a "burning platform" for making the mental switch …

Still, sooner or later the moment of truth arrives: rising costs combined with sales that are (still) too low imply that the "technology heaven" period should be closed and that the switch toward professional marketing and sales must be made. What becomes clear then is that different and larger funding is needed to launch this reorientation. Boosting sales doesn't happen easily and requires significant efforts and resources. This awakening often occurs when the company is making this step from startup to scale-up—one could in a way say from technology focus to market focus.

Most startups discover that regardless how fantastic their product or service is in their eyes, the real battle will be in the market, where customers have alternatives or are not making this "new thing" a top priority in their supply diversification …

The search for money

Here then we have the startup ready to make the step toward a scale-up: the product or service is (kind of) mature, sales are (slowly) starting but the seed money (and possibly Series A and also Series B capital) are almost consumed ... Obviously, the Alarm Bell Procedure has been launched (once or twice) and tensions are mounting in the company, the Board, and in the shareholders' meeting ... On top of that, it becomes clear that in order to boost sales, extra funding will be needed (one should also not overlook the increase of working capital, almost always a consequence of growth). So the time is ripe for a Series C funding round—or so it seems.

So what are the options? And how should one handle this?

The first step (see for an overview of steps see Addendum 6) is obviously to readdress the company's strategy. Has our vision / mission changed, or do we keep on going for the same objectives? Is everybody still aligned around this (shareholders, Board, management, founders)? This needs to be clearly agreed upon before moving any further: the capital round will be a disaster if the investor sees discordance on the future direction in his contacts with company representatives: one needs to know where one is going.

Next, it is necessary to update or rewrite the company's business plan and financial plan of the company. No doubt new insights will have to be incorporated into the mostly overoptimistic approach that existed at the beginning ... From the cash flow planning, it should become clear what over the years will be the lowest (negative) point in the cash situation. In order to have some flexibility, I would recommend to go for a funding of some 150 percent of that lowest point.

Now follows the question of the type of funding. At the risk of sounding too orthodox in my financial thinking, a company and its Board will have to distinguish whether the funding serves a long-term need of the company or if it merely helps bridge a period after which easy payback will be possible. In my view (also considering the long-term need for more working capital that will not disappear), the company almost always needs to provide for a long-term financial need. In that case loans, or at least bank loans and similar, are not the most recommended route, no matter how financially sound the balance sheet may be. A different "loan" option (see further) involves so-called CLAs (convertible loan agreement), but most of the time the company needs additional risk capital, plain and simple.

So a capital round: How do you go about this? As usual, preparation is everything and urgency is not really the best environment … Here is some advice: take a year as a good estimate of the time that will be needed to close the round properly. One lesson learned over the last years is that the mood of the capital markets can substantially change over even relatively short times: one better be prepared … Also: whether one likes it or not, a capital round has a lot of similarities with an ordinary sales process. The company "comes on the market" not really to be sold but still to be attractive to investors. Professional, respectful, and (better) humble communication is helpful here.

This is why business plan and financial plan need to be (also) reworked into an attractive Investment of Information Memorandum, preferably complemented with a one page Teaser highlighting the major attractive points for the investor. As well known in marketing communication, these documents need to be appealing in the eyes of the investors, not in the eyes of the founders … Some help might be welcome (see further).

First question: Who handles what? Obviously, within the framework of governance the Board will de minimis have to see if the continuity of the company is not in danger and that progress is made in the raising of funds. It will also have to work out with the management an alternative plan to keep the company afloat if the funding does not materialize as expected. The Board will have to be kept in the loop when negotiations start, as it is more than likely that the company represented by the Board will be cosignatory to the final deal.

Although the final approval of a capital raise (and the associated conditions) is a matter for the shareholders, common practice dictates that the founders (which normally includes the CEO) take the lead in the search, possibly assisted by the Chair of the Board or some other Board members with experience in such endeavors. The reason is simple: the founders represent–or should represent–the essence of the company. Not to be overlooked is that investors invest as much (or even more) in the (leading) people of the company as in their product or service ...

A capital round is an exceptional and complicated process and getting it right requires at least considering specialized assistance. For example, the help of specialized lawyers is crucial from the start (they may already, for example, be involved in drafting the NDA (nondisclosure agreement)). Possibly one day AI is going to be of help, but I would not bet on this 100 percent, as errors in these proceedings are paid dearly. Penny wise, pound foolish ... More debatable is the use of investment bankers or M&A boutiques: in my experience as these capital rounds are mostly below 10 Mio €, their involvement could be overkill (and over expensive) in some ways. It all depends ...

How then to approach the capital market? There is plenty of information on the internet on all sorts of risk capital providers. There is an incredible variety of funds, individuals, corporations, government agencies, crowd funding, etc., that one could possibly address, both in this country and abroad. Here I have learned that in fact a thorough reflection of the Board is needed on the type of investor before storming the capital markets. The reason is simple: the ambitions / priorities of the investor need to align with those of the company. At the stage of a scale-up it is most probably advisable to prioritize investors with a longer-term horizon. But the search implies more than the time horizon of the investor: it includes the investor's priority areas (such as sustainability, specific fields such as IT, just to mention the "hottest") but also the startup's wishes in terms of getting additional "skills" within its shareholder group. Such a definition of "most preferred investor" will prove to be a substantial help in the success of the round. Addressing the "wrong" investors will unavoidably result is a lot of refusals and ruin the image of the startup's capital search—as usual, bad news travels fast and the investors do not live in isolated towers ...

There now follows the long and often frustrating tour of (selected) investors to find the right one(s)— maintaining courage has definitely been a challenge over the most recent period, but in the end it is always the same: if one stops, it is over and finished. So the only option is to continue. Anyway, in the best of circumstances one ends up with some two or three candidates, who will get the opportunity to present a letter of intent or a nonbinding offer. There then follows the step of selecting the best candidate, more often than not on the basis of their valuation of the company. A point of advice is also to take the knowledge of the investor with regard to local regulations and practices into account—nobody really needs additional complications in this area. An intermediate remark: I always prefer to keep the discussion on the valuation of the company to the last stage of negotiations, rather than putting it, for example, already in the information memorandum.

For the sake of completeness: I have not discussed the opportunities with regard to subsidies in this section. Obviously, they should be looked at continuously, but any startup will face the moment when "real" risk capital will be needed to boost its further development and growth.

Closing the deal

There are a lot of administrative steps and documents to be drafted in a capital round (see addendum 6), but before that, agreement needs to be found on the essentials of the deal. That normally takes the form of a Term Sheet, and if that is well made, specialist lawyers, accountants, and so forth should be able to work out the full documentation. Over the last decades I have witnessed a staggering growth in the amount of pages of such documents, reflecting the growing number of conditions and stipulations in these agreements. While understanding such copious output for much bigger and complicated deals, one wonders if, for these all in all limited deals, such expansion in volume and complexity has really brought an equivalent added value to the signatories ... Anyway, the toughest negotiation element in 95 percent of the cases is no doubt the valuation of the company (that is essentially pre-money—which means before the capital raise, or post-money, that is, after the capital raise), as it will define the number of shares the new investors will receive for their money. Obviously, existing shareholders would like the valuation to be as high as possible, whereas new investors aim for the reverse. Nota bene: a particular situation arises when some of the historical investors also join the round ... To say the least: most of the time such a situation is not easy to resolve ... What are the solutions for getting out of this? First of all, such a deal is composed of many elements (including liquidation preferences, representation, dividend distribution, drag along, tag along, etc.) and it is on the global deal that an agreement needs to be found.

Another solution might be to review the share allocation after reaching (or not reaching) certain targets in the future. And last but not least: a Convertible Loan Agreement can be set up, leaving the valuation issue essentially to the next capital round. I have two bits of advice concerning this: first get through the discussions now and "do it right the first time," and second, try to keep it as simple as possible. Practice shows that holding up all the conditions written down in such agreements is not really possible for small units such as startups or scale-ups ... And in some cases a (much) lower valuation has to be accepted in the end: such a down-round is never pleasant but occasionally the best solution.

The new reality

So let's take for the sake of simplicity that the capital injection just described coincides with the shift from startup to scale-up. Frequently—and given the new more substantial capital injections—this results in a more "professional" and demanding governance of the company. Those who have invested before in proper Corporate Governance will now highly benefit from earlier efforts. For others, the new reality will be rather a surprise and possibly awkward. So what does this new reality look like?

First of all, the stakes are substantially more important than before and imply a much more rigorous control by the Board over the progress of the company. Experimental freedom makes room for disciplined execution. The new investors are interested in seeing the (financial) promises made materialize. One must realize that the nature of the investors changes when moving from "seed" investors to more financial growth investors, like VC and family funds. As a consequence, this is also typically the time when the selection of some sort of CFO person of function becomes necessary. Reporting will have to become spotless and accurate. Additionally, it is also frequently the moment where an official auditor is engaged to check the accounts of the company so as to include this report on the consolidated financial statements in the annual shareholders' meeting. Anyway, more than likely the emphasis on whatever is financial will tend to grow substantially.

Second and linked to the first point is the shift in power. It depends somewhat on the percentage of shares the new investors have acquired, but the important dominance of the management-founders in the first years now shifts in the hands of the Board. In itself there is no problem in such a shift (which sometimes is even overdue), as long as everybody stays on his side of the governance. Although the position of the management might as from now become a point of discussion, the split of responsibilities and tasks between Board and management has to be upheld. Also, within the management a more strict definition of who does what and who has which authority will become evident. The time of everybody does kind of everything will be over.

A third, more tricky point, linked to the preceding one ... It is not uncommon that in these faster growth circumstances (or a bit later) the question is raised if the CEO (still typically at that moment the founder or one of the founders) is still the right person to lead the company. This is a highly sensitive question but also a highly relevant one. The qualities and focus required from the "number one" must adapt to the new reality or at least new balance: from largely exploratory / creative / dynamic, the culture often has to shift into a more consolidation / professionalization / stabilization mode, and not all startup CEOs are able to evolve toward this new horizon. The focus has to shift from development to scaling up, and that can call on different talent. On top of that, the Board will have to understand that more power will have to be delegated to the CEO, involving more stress on his or her agenda. The Board has a particularly difficult role to play here, as often the company is extremely attached to the personality of the founder. But whether a CEO is OK or not OK depends often more on the situation the company is in than on the intrinsic personal qualities of the person. They simply have to match: that's the key thing. And the Board must, within the principles of Corporate Governance take the best decision in the interests of all stakeholders.

Fourth: the Board needs to step up its governance professionalism. The points highlighted in the startup period have more than likely not always been fully implemented. This is now the time to get this completed. Be it in the area of Board competences, diversity, structure, operation, evaluation, etc., things now have to really be brought up to standard. If new Board members are selected, a good onboarding process of that Board member should be in place, where the director receives a thorough information pack with all the critical information needed to profoundly understand the various aspects of the company. Who are the key people (executives, other board members, shareholders), who are the critical external value chain partners (suppliers, customers, other key actors), what is the current strategy and business model, what is the financial health, etc.

And the quality impetus does not end with recruitment: the directors should dedicate time and effort to continuously update their skills and knowledge. This can also be done through internal or external trainings of presentations by executives, or by external education providers.

In a startup, one might get the impression that the founders are building the plane while flying it; in a scale-up, the plane will have to become certified to sustain gusty breezes before taking off again …

7

BEST PRACTICES

Looking at the many challenges and pitfalls facing startups and scale-ups, what are the best practices in terms of Governance in general and Board operation in particular? Based on my experience, I would like to list the following points.

Focus

A startup being by definition a dynamic and creative environment, the danger of going for yet another different target or direction every month/quarter or so is very real. Under the pressure of trying to score rapidly and impressively, the temptation to instantly drop a not-so-successful option or route can be dangerously high. By this I do not wish to imply that unsuccessful initiatives need to be followed through eternally, but rather that if switching is envisaged, it should preferably be done after analysis so that a lesson can be drawn from it. A strategy definition, based on the company's articles of association and in particular on its mission, is thus extremely important—for those who have an allergy for the word strategy, let's just call it "where do we want to go and how do we get there." Once this has been defined and set, it should not be changed without good cause: in fact, without this focus the company will be lost. That focus is something the Board should be the guardian of. Before changing the direction of actions, one should at least be able to identify the reason why the changed course holds better chances for success. Too often urgency prevails over quality at the detriment of longer-term success. Again this does not constitute an invitation for a passive Board; rather, it is a call for a Board that makes sure checks are conducted before dropping old maps and switching to new horizons.

A practical way of conducting such checks is to agree on a set of KPIs (key performance indicators) that are regularly reported by management and allow the Board to keep track of the progress in executing the annual plan. Such annual plans are obviously intrinsically linked with the strategy: they detail what will be the main areas of attention and effort in that year to execute the strategy. Keeping focus means a certain formality in reporting, I am afraid ...

By the time a startup reaches the level of a scale-up, the above should be considered a given. The time of endlessly seeking perfection and upgrading should have shifted toward a much more disciplined execution of the agreed-upon business plan. Obviously this requires a different mindset from all the key people in the company and it happens that at this moment some managers or even founders leave to explore other, more adventurous horizons.

Cash

Even more than a regular company, a startup needs to monitor the cash position very carefully. This implies not only the actual cash position but also the one in the future.

The most frequent "surprise" in startups is the sudden appearance of a dramatic cash situation. An attentive follow-up of cash evolution is therefore mandatory. The Board plays an important role here, as entrepreneurs have repeatedly been shown to be overly optimistic when it comes to cash needs and cash bleeds—a particular example here being working capital needs. Especially in a situation where the company needs extra funding, there is a world of difference between a company standing against the wall being fully cash-strapped and a company well ahead of the emergency status. It should not be forgotten that the thing that really brings a startup to the end of its journey is the absence of cash and liquidity …

As a consequence, the high quality of not only the actual cash situation but even more so of expected cash evolution is key. I will return to this matter.

The above priority does not disappear when moving into a scale-up, although it might become less of an urgent problem given the probably more comfortable financial situation and the improved financial management. Still, the basics will stand …

The customer

As hard as it may be for entrepreneurs, one has to admit that in many cases only a very small group of people or companies are really eagerly "waiting" for the new service or product the startup is bringing on the market. Facing the unavoidable difficulties of introducing a new product or service to the market, the same entrepreneurs are frequently tempted to blame the targeted customers for being too conservative, too passive, or simply just too stupid to understand the incredible benefits their invention is going to bring them. In those cases it is time for the Board to bring them "back to earth" and in particular stress the basic principle that "the customer is always right." The Board should really realize that the company's success will ultimately result from its sales and that the most crucial actor in this process is the customer. Accordingly, the Board should as far as necessary be the advocate of a genuine interest in and the importance of the customers. Understanding profoundly the reason why a customer says no to an offer is crucial (just as much as understanding a successful sale and why he or she says yes). Documenting all this is the right way to start a continuous improvement program based on customer feedback.

Obviously the attention to the customer remains paramount when the startup moves into the scale-up phase. As the company grows and establishes a more stable and wider customer base, more sophisticated techniques will become mandatory, such as measuring more explicitly customer feedback, competitive activity, pricing policy, promotional initiatives, and so forth. The growth and extension of sales will be the key challenge for the scale-up, and customer centricity will be an absolute must.

Human Capital

No doubt a startup cannot be a success without a good USP (unique selling proposition), be it a concept, a product, or a service that is realistic and in which a lot of customers will show interest. That being said, and provided funding has been found, it is equally true that the USP will not become a success without the appropriate contribution, efforts, commitments, and skills of dedicated staff. This is more easily said than done. Obviously, everything starts with the selection of people. Given the age of the entrepreneurs-managers, it should come as no surprise that their experience in interviewing and selecting people is not yet very high. Some appropriate guidance from the Board is recommended in this process, as well as the involvement of a professional recruitment office in the selection. Young managers often underestimate the engagement (financial and other) the company takes on in engaging people … Obviously, the development of the right human capital does not stop at recruitment. If you want new people to become part of the team, a little introduction program is advisable. We are not talking about weeks of training but rather of an intensive talk with the CEO where she or he explains to the recruit the purpose of the company, its values and culture, the basics of its organization, and last but not least what is expected from the new employee. In the following years, attention should be given to the development of the employee, possibly through education or rotation, as fits best. A satisfactory remuneration package should ensure they don't leave just for money (this may possibly include share options, as explained further). It should not be forgotten, however, that money does not motivate (or a least not for a long time): the only risk is demotivation.

The shifts involved in moving to a scale-up also impact the human capital of the company. As highlighted before, a more sales-driven organization is in order and in addition to bringing in more sales personnel, it will reset the priorities and culture of the company. Pushing technology evolution now becomes secondary to achieving revenue growth. To oversimplify the point: engineers will have to be replaced by sales professionals. For some companies, this can come as a shock, especially if the founders-managers are of the type of the eternal inventor. Within the framework of good governance, the Board will have no option but to handle this appropriately and possibly change people. And not to forget what was also indicated earlier: a stronger financial / reporting function will have to be set up.

Unfortunately, startups and scale-ups—like other companies—also lose people, sometimes willingly, sometimes unwillingly. Rather than just a "goodbye and all the best," this opportunity should be grasped through organizing a good exit interview (preferably by the CEO), in order to find out what could be learned from this departure.

Financial reporting

The sooner a startup starts with a good financial reporting system, the better. Somebody inside or outside the company should be clearly accountable and competent to conduct the financial reporting. In practice this is mostly done by an external accountant; however, the particularities of the startup should be explained and detailed to her/him and if possible the accountant should be of sufficiently high level to support and carry through operations such as capital rounds and other steps in the growth of the startup. Amortization and depreciation rules need to be specifically agreed upon and respected. Needless to say, some form of discipline is needed for this, meaning among other things a good follow-up of in- and outgoing invoices, contracts, commitments, and so forth. As for any reporting system, rubbish in means rubbish out.

In terms of what needs to be reported, a classical profit and loss statement should do (see Addendum 3). Next to the actual figures of a certain period (could be monthly or quarterly) and the year-to-date (YTD) ones, it is advisable to also give the corresponding figures of the same figures for the same year and compare them to the established annual budget. In this context, it should be stressed that an annual plan/budget is of fundamental importance for any startup. The fact that reality is always different from a plan should not minimize the relevance of setting a reference for the next year and thus also starting a learning process in improving planning the future for the company. Last but not least, the financial reporting should include a forward estimate of how the year should end based on the information available at the moment of reporting (year-end-outlook or YEO/L). The proposed table thus allows the Board to look on one table at actual performance, compare it with the past and the budget, and have a forward-looking estimate of future performance.

Referring to the paragraph above on cash, financial reporting cannot be complete without a proper view on the cash situation of the company as well as of the future evolution of that same situation. Obviously, the future here is more important than the past or the plan: the cash situation is crucial for the continuity of the company. An occasionally overlooked element in cash need estimating is the sometimes surprisingly quick-growing working capital need when a company starts expanding its sales and production. Depending on the nature of the business, the costs of making the products or services come months ahead of the receipt of the payment of the invoices sent to the customers after delivery.

As a final motivation for high-quality financial reporting, it cannot be stressed enough that investors are very averse to (negative) surprises in the company's financial performance and that their willingness to further financially support the startup depends very much on trust built on high-quality information.

Everything stated here fully applies to the scale-up as well, but to a more significant degree. No more room anymore for incomplete, overdue, incorrect, etc. financial reporting: the strongest discipline is what is needed at this stage. It will even more than before be essential to maintain trust and confidence of the investors in what the company is accomplishing. Since it is not excluded that after the scale-up more capital will be needed, the better way to go should be clear.

Effectiveness and efficiency

Startups are highly creative environments, and so they should be. Freedom to experiment and try out new/better things is intrinsic to the genes of startups. It is also what makes the working environment very attractive to employees with the entrepreneurial and creative spirit needed to make the company a success. Most of the time, the original idea leading to the creation of the startup comes out of a pretty unstructured, loose, no risk, sometimes chaotic environment. From the hobby garage to the PhD thesis, from the old boys' network to a simple coincidence or conversation, concepts, inventions, innovations, developments, improvements, etc. can pop up and be further explored and developed so as to lead to the creation of a company to make the idea or product a business success. But when the company is constituted (and certainly when this is done with new financiers), the music changes. Virtually from one day to the other, the entrepreneurs/founders (and their Board) face a situation where budgets, timing, strategy, targets, organization, and so on make their entrance. Although unavoidable, making that switch is a difficult task for any company. While on the one hand the company needs to conserve this "free" entrepreneurial and creative environment, on the other it must learn to adequately include effectiveness and efficiency in what it is doing. If not, the company is at high risk of missing its commitments in terms of performance versus plan and budget. Furthermore, a number of additional tasks are to be accomplished—preferably equally effectively and efficiently. For a startup with most of the time not extremely experienced entrepreneurs-founders-managers on the Board, this can be a hard nut to crack. Once again a good Governance structure can be of substantial help here. It is the Board that needs to monitor and stimulate such shifts, including deciding on needed training and external support if such is mandatory.

Again for a scale-up the phase of the hobby-garage-entrepreneur-inventor-founder should be closed off. This not only revolves around—possibly different—people (see above) but also implies the required systems and procedures. The Board should guide and control the implementation of the appropriate tools to fulfill these requirements. I am referring to subjects such as budgeting, investment planning, compensation systems, recruitment procedures, quality management, expenses' management, environmental policy, communication priorities, etc.

When to start

One could argue that installing a proper Corporate Governance is not a first-line, top priority for a startup company. There are arguments for this: so many things to do to get the company going, so many meetings to attend, so many papers to finish, so many people to see, etc. Although understandable, these arguments do not hold up against the benefits of doing things right the first time. Corporate Governance and all the practical consequences following from its application as described in this publication—should be considered from the start as an essential part of the well-being of the company.

On top of this principle, it is not difficult to understand that the longer one waits for implementation, the more laborious it will be to get all Governance matters sorted, not to mention the corrections that will have to be made related to the possible "false start." To be clear: Corporate Governance should be implemented into the startup from its inception, and if at all possible the necessary steps to improve it further should be started early on.

To be clear on the next scale-up phase: I would consider it to be close to impossible to engage in a professional scale-up capital round without proper Corporate Governance installed in the company—there is just no way around that.

Compliance

Whether pleasant or not, a startup or a scale-up is just as any company required to respect all applicable rules and regulations as set in legislation. This is a considerable task, and it occurs frequently that this is not directly the number one priority of the management (and the Board) of a startup, to put it mildly. This is understandable but also inefficient and dangerous. It is inefficient because whether one likes it or not, conformity with law will have to be achieved at one moment in time but very likely with a very much higher cost and effort than if it had been done right the first time. It is dangerous not only because of the possible fines but also because of the damaged reputation of the company (in a narrower or broader circle, depending on the violation). Let's not forget that many of these regulations make perfect sense, even for a startup (example: safety at work regulations).

The basic elements of legal compliance are given in Addendum 4. In practice a good legal firm, a social secretariat, and an explicit and strong commitment from the top of the company should cover most of these challenges, although once again the Board should equally keep an eye on this and intervene in an appropriate way if necessary. Indeed, as a professional Director knows, her or his responsibility can be involved in these matters also. So on compliance with rules and regulations I can be very short. There is just zero choice, be it a startup or a scale-up: just do it.

To conclude this section: payment terms and the timing of suppliers' invoices and salaries are equally set by law (if not agreed differently). Although salaries are generally handled appropriately (through the social secretariat in most cases), it is a widely spread disease in startups to be unprofessional with respect to the timing of supplier invoice payments. This should be avoided. The importance of suppliers in the success of a startup is often grossly underestimated and accordingly a startup should show them respect in honoring legal (or contractual) invoice payment terms. It will be crucial for the reputation of the startup and for the priority and goodwill it gets from its suppliers.

ESG

ESG (Environment, Social, Governance) has gained considerable attention over the last years. The concept strives to properly balance financial results, transparency, social interests, and corporate governance. A formal reporting on these priorities is in the planning stages on the EU level, and there are several ESG frameworks for reporting this type of information, but this falls outside the scope of this book. Although the mandatory reporting will initially be limited to bigger and/or stock market–listed companies, a discussion is also relevant for startups and certainly for scale-ups.

The first reason is that this is just the way to go. Companies exclusively interested in the financial bottom line will never continue to be successful in the long run. In fact, ESG was and is in essence already embedded in proper Corporate Governance. It now becomes more important and is more detailed in its particular requirements than in the past.

The second reason is that the ESG obligations will simply trickle down from the bigger companies into the smaller ones. Business customers will increasingly demand ESG reporting from their (even small) suppliers—but very similar concerns could come from retail customers or their associations. And other company stakeholders will get interested too ...

The third reason is that attracting capital will become very difficult if ESG is not part of the company's genes. More often than not, this is already happening in the practice I have seen: still informally most of the time (meaning investors themselves checking ESG points) but no doubt it will become a formal request soon.

So how to handle this in a startup and how to improve it in a scale-up transition?

Although from a formal perspective ESG is a reporting duty, a start-up should first of all make sure its basic values and culture embrace the three ESG areas.

In fact, a startup should have a clear vision statement and mission, balancing the interests of the bottom-line, the environment, and society. This statement or mission should lead the company to appropriately develop services or products that are profitable to all stakeholders. There is a particular opportunity a startup should not miss here: it is at the start that it is easiest to set the culture and values of the company.

As a next stage, it is advisable to think of ways to set targets and quantify some of the priorities addressed in the mission. With regard to environment, obviously the previously discussed compliance point needs to be stressed again. But probably an obvious reference could be climate change impact reduction. Additionally, anything relating to circularity could get a place here from the beginning.

On the social level, I can only once again stress the importance of proper safety management as well as the importance of the human capital (including not only development but also mutual respect, inclusivity, equity, privacy, etc.), both handled also repeatedly elsewhere in this book.

And of course, holding it all together is proper Governance itself—meaning making sure priorities, systems, controls, procedures, etc. are sufficiently in place to uphold the set ESG principles and targets.

Needless to say, starting such an ESG process (or let's call it paying attention to ESG early on) will not only benefit later reporting and development but will also have a beneficial effect on the company's financial results.

In conclusion and in my own experience, it all starts at the very beginning of a startup by a clear definition of what the purpose of the company really is. That definition should embrace more interests than those of the shareholders and thus build the proper company culture and set the appropriate values. If well formulated, it can not only last for a very long time but will also be extremely beneficial to all stakeholders.

8

ATTENTION POINTS

Keeping balances

A startup by definition faces a serious number of challenges and choices— possibly even larger and more complicated than an "established" company. The need for focus has been stressed before, but considering the many options and questions, it is clear that not all matters might get focus. It is all a matter of setting priorities and in doing so, balance is essential. Governance structures play an important role in this process. An incomplete set of areas where balance is of particular importance is given below.

The first balance which needs to be respected is the one between the short and the long term. In a startup fires abound, and it is tempting (and sometimes necessary) to turn the entire team into firefighters. But tackling only short-term problems could be detrimental to the longer term success of the startup. A proper Governance structure and in particular the Board of Directors must provide the required balance in discussing and orienting both short-term and long-term issues. If this balance is overlooked, the company might face nasty surprises because future evolutions have not properly been discussed, handled, and reflected in an appropriate strategy. In the scale-up situation, the balance obviously shifts (or should shift) more to the long- and midterm. A good annual plan and its firm execution are the best guarantees for getting out the permanent fire-fighting mode.

The second balance is the one between the different stakeholders, where especially the interaction between founders-entrepreneurs-shareholders-managers on one side and the external shareholders-investors on the other is a tricky one. The former group's main interest is most likely to build a company where they can prosper for a good part of the rest of their career; for the latter, the matter of a successful exit in a five to seven years' time frame often is more relevant. Those two basically different aspirations can lead to serious upsets in the company in general and on the Board in particular if not handled properly. Transparency is key here, and again an independent Chairman can be a good option. Another important stakeholder is personnel. Their commitment is crucial to the success of the company, and in terms of their compensation the question of allocation of share options or other long-term incentive plans linked to participating in the company's equity is a matter of considerable importance. Obviously, a shareholders' agreement will have to be obtained but again an independent Board should be best placed to be a good judge on the plusses and minuses for the company of installing such a system (which in my very personal view sometimes brings a lot more work than real long-term benefits, but I admit opinions may vary in this respect).

A particular point of interest is the relationship with the founder(s): he/she or they did not start the company to become experts in or champions of Corporate Governance. Their key values and interests revolve around creativity, freedom, growth, etc. and these should be considered and above all be respected by the Governance structures. Again the role of the Chair is crucial here in making sure that agility is still possible within the good rules of Governance. This is possible, but requires quite extensive attention and communication.

Maybe one last odd reflection on the above: the Board thus needs to operate as a group focusing essentially on the interests of the company, without being dominated by one single individual. That works better if Board meetings take place at a neutral location—this could be the company seat (which would be standard) but preferably not the offices of one particular Board member.

When moving to the scale-up, the impact of the (new) external investors is likely to increase, also on the Board. Again, balance will have to be found, guided by the principle that on a Board nobody represents a particular shareholder; rather, all members are merely appointed to that Board to exclusively serve the best interests of the company.

The third balance in the company relates to the structure of the balance sheet. In particular, the company should be attentive to financing the long-term capital needs by long-term liabilities such as equity and long-term loans. Working capital needs are often not considered as long-term funding needs or are at least underestimated, whereas in most cases they are there to stay. Obviously, many early-day shareholders will not be too eager to see their percentage in the company go down with a possible equity increase brought in by new shareholders, especially when in many cases such funding rounds happen in the so-called valley of death where the valuation of the company may not seem as attractive as it was at the founding date, with all the consequences for the first shareholders …

As indicated before, the startup capital need to move to a scale-up is best solved by risk capital being brought into the company. Any professional investor will comply with this. Overleveraging is not the wisest financial strategy even for a startup or scale-up with a high potential, … the black swan might still be just around the corner …

The fourth balance concerns the necessity to maintain a creative, entrepreneurial free spirit and atmosphere in the company on the one hand while on the other managing and controlling the company through instruments such as budgets, reports, procedures, etc. Once a company has been set up, the latter principle becomes unavoidable, whereas the former necessity can be and often is essential for the growth of the company. The fact that financial resources are always limited, however, makes it necessary to stay in control of what is happening. That can be done in a remote way, at arm's length, by allowing "creativity with a purpose" to evolve within a given framework. A lot will depend on the personalities of the people involved in this debate, but with some goodwill things can be straightened out ...

More focus on management and control when shifting to the scale-up phase is unavoidable. Obviously, depending on the type of product or service, further developments could be required or even essential, but it is more than probable that these also will have to be structured and planned in a more rigid way. With increasing financial and business risks, a closer management and control in these areas will be unavoidable.

Communication

It may seem strange and even inappropriate to discuss "communication" in a publication discussing Corporate Governance. However, it is important for a startup (and later in a scale-up) to get this right, although it is frequently somewhat neglected—including the role the Board has to play.

The first important group in this field are the shareholders, in particular those not included in the Board of Directors (and they can constitute a big group, like with crowd funding). Many things happen in a startup, hopefully a lot as planned but possibly even more not really as planned or hoped for. As has been said, the world of a startup is full of surprises ... It is clear that management— and probably to a somewhat lesser extent the Board of Directors—are aware of these unexpected events. However, a large group of other shareholders no doubt shares a need for knowing how the company (and their investment) is doing. This communication need cannot be fulfilled with just one annual meeting of the shareholders as foreseen in the law (the AGM or annual general meeting). Given the dynamics in a startup, too many—sometimes crucial— things happen in such a short time that a more intense communication with shareholders is advisable.

A solution is to publish a short quarterly shareholder information letter covering the most important events, combined with a simplified financial statement. Next to this a face-to-face meeting with all shareholders could be organized every six months or so to give them the regular opportunity to ask for clarification of the company's situation and inquire about future plans.

Needless to say, shareholders need to be appropriately respected for having believed in the company through their investment, but next to that it is in many cases their positive interest that will determine the success of any future capital round. New investors always carefully watch the willingness of the original shareholders to invest before themselves taking such a step.

As a last comment in relation to shareholder communication, it should be stressed that such communication should preferably be validated by the Board of Directors, given the direct Governance relationship between shareholders and the Board.

For a scale-up—especially if new investors have substantially stepped in—a more strict reporting to shareholders will probably be a part of the (new) shareholders' agreement.

A second important group in terms of communication are the company employees. As stated before, management is (or at least should be ...) very informed on what is happening and where things are going. Although startups have in general a pretty limited staff, these employees are not always as well informed as one would conclude from the size of the company. However, their commitment and drive depend also on being involved in the company and that is impossible without adequate information on the company. It is therefore advisable to set up a structured communication with staff—a good example is the CEO talking on a monthly basis to all staff about where the company is, where it should be going, and how staff will be instrumental in achieving these goals. Needless to say, for home office employees (of whom we see more and more) such structured information is crucially important. The Board can and should be occasionally involved in this communication with employees, be it on a more informal basis.

The intention is not to "jump over the head of the CEO" but rather to complement where needed. Directors in general and the Chairman in particular should not "hide" away; rather, they should be available for employee contact, while maintaining and stressing the role and authority of the CEO and her or his management.

As the company becomes a scale-up and (in all likelihood) grows the number of employees, this internal communication becomes even more crucial and needs to be stepped up and formalized. A monthly socializing moment with the CEO giving a state of affairs of the company to all personnel is a good move. Next to that, engaging to involve a maximum of people in a more bottom-up budget exercise could also contribute to spreading relevant company information and helping people to understand the challenges ahead and their commitment needed to overcome them.

A third group for communication is the public at large and authorities and related in particular. A company oriented toward a B2C basis will have no problem understanding that addressing the public at large is of fundamental importance to their success. It might be less obvious to B2B companies, but here some particular segments of the public are important. Startups must, like all companies, deserve their right to operate and that includes transparency and openness to the public: startup or not. There are several ways to get this going, but membership in an adequate employers' organization might be a good start. Next to this, a startup depends on the goodwill and support of authorities and regulators. This involves getting the required permits and approvals, but it needs to be remembered also that quite a few startups are beneficiaries of generous subsidies from governmental and related structures.

Communicating with them in an appropriate way—and preferably not only when there is a big problem and you need their help—is therefore advisable. It will depend from company to company how to set it up in practice, suffice here to stress the relevancy. A particular segment of the public are neighbors. It is good to know who works next to you, and you can never have too many supporters ...

Directors can be involved on an invitation basis in contacts with authorities in cases where their influence can be of service to the management.

No surprise: the same applies to scale-ups, obviously.

A fourth group, occasionally forgotten, are the people closely involved with the company (be it startup or scale-up) and important if not essential to its success. I am referring here to the rather diverse group of (key) material suppliers, long-standing consultants or freelancers, lawyers, external accountants, etc. The contributions of these groups—commonly known as "stakeholders" alongside shareholders, customers, the public and the employees—are rather frequently only recognized when suddenly they are no longer available, for one reason or another. Meanwhile, it goes without saying that one would expect stronger relationships and more efficient cooperation if these individuals are informed on the status of the startup or scale-up they are working for. How to set up such communication is not obvious. As a minimal effort, the key contact in the company should at least now and then discuss the state of affairs informally with their external counterpart.

Last but not least: the customers. Obviously, communication efforts are very specific to the type of customers the company is targeting. Most startups understand the need to approach potential customers and use more or less appropriate means to get to them. Again, the diversity is too large and spending money here should be carefully planned and monitored. It cannot be repeated enough that the key challenge of a startup and even more a scale-up is in the end not to "develop" but to "sell"—from this perspective communication takes on great importance. Given the centrality of customers, Board members should not hesitate to join staff in contacts with key customers: understanding customers can only improve decision-making in this area.

9

LESSONS LEARNED ...

The do's and don'ts

Based on my experience, I guess it boils down to the following key points to remember:

Do's:

- do set up (and write it in the articles of association) a high quality Corporate Governance structure involving a professional Board of Directors
- do give attention to the composition of the Board, in particular making sure there is sufficient independence to assure the real responsibility of the Board is followed through (which is not achieved through the representation of the interest of one shareholder by one Director)
- do support the nomination of a competent and preferably independent Chair of the Board
- do make sure entrepreneurs/founders and investors are fully aligned on the longer-term future of the company (also exit and related matters)
- try to get Directors with experience in startup and scale-up Governance or hands-on experience of being on a startup/ scale-up Board themselves.

- make sure Board members understand that they are on the Board to serve exclusively the best interest of the company they are a Board member of (and not the interest of a particular shareholder)

Don'ts:

- do not confuse an advisory Board with a Board of Directors. Because of its genuine involvement and responsibility, the latter is preferred over the former. This does not mean that an advisory Board is something bad, a Board of Directors is just structurally better from a Governance point of view, and as it is mandated by law anyway ...
- do not accept lower values and quality standards than in other companies
- do not engage as a Board into "managing" the company but keep on your side of the field: management and Board have a clearly different role and responsibility— all functions better when these are mutually respected
- do not get into a firefighting mode on the Board as much as possible
- do not be afraid or ashamed to get external help and don't aim too low in quality: it does not need to be cheap because it is a startup: it needs to achieve acceptable quality, and as we know: "penny wise, pound foolish"

Ride the storms

It is certainly not excluded by any divine law or other rule that a startup or scale-up can enjoy an evolution that is absolutely smooth, well controlled, hassle free, perfectly monitored, absolutely consistent with plans … Unfortunately, I still have to come across one …

On the contrary, most of the time we see that startups are full of unexpected events, some more catastrophic than others. As Mr. Murphy[7] stated regarding accidents, "anything that can go wrong will go wrong and if it does, it will go wrong at the most inappropriate moment." … In my own experience, I have witnessed fights between entrepreneurs/founders almost leading to completely paralyzing the company, legal action of shareholders against the company, customers not respecting their engagements, authorities taking strong action against the company, extremely aggressive actions of competitors, (very big) surprises in financial performance and cash evolution (following sometimes hidden accounting figures), banks not taking up their commitments, key people leaving the company, shareholders defaulting on their promises, suppliers completely missing their delivery schedules, delays in permits and authorizations, and so on and so forth. The list is endless and on top of that quite unpredictable, in nature, size, time, etc.

Needless to say that in such circumstances the easy way out is just quitting and calling it a day. That is, however, not really what the successful startups generally do (and even less the scale-ups, obviously). Whatever the challenge and obviously within the borders of regulations and legislation as well as the articles of association

7 Edward Aloysius Murphy Jr. (January 11, 1918–July 17, 1990): American aviation engineer, expert in safety systems and management.

of the company, they never give up, learn from their mistakes, and go on. That kind of attitude should also be a quality of the Board of Directors and of course of the management, obviously while respecting legal provisions for companies in trouble (alarm bell procedure, etc.). Also one needs to keep the feet on the ground: if the ship is really lost, evacuation is the only possible solution. But most of the time this is not necessary, as it is surprising how many solutions one can find for a seemingly hopeless situation if one looks carefully enough … And there are more helping hands around than one would expect … and as Winston Churchill once said: when you're going through hell, keep going …

10

CONCLUSIONS

The need for having appropriate Governance in startups and scale-ups is more and more acknowledged and is gaining ground in Belgium and abroad. That is a very welcome development. The experience in doing so in the best way possible is growing but it should be clear that it must be different from bigger companies in order to make it workable and efficient. But although Governance in startups and scale-ups is different and specific, one should also realize that the core principles of good Corporate Governance apply to any company. This booklet has the ambition to clarify somewhat the distinctions that need to be made, in particular in the context of the limited means of startups and scale-ups. Still, I firmly believe Corporate Governance is crucial for the long-term success of a start-up and scale-up. Corporate Governance promotes confidence and thus facilitates investment interest.

For Directors a concluding remark might also be that their involvement in these cases is more direct: the extensive lack of experience and resources implies a much more hands-on approach from Board members—obviously, maintaining the independence of the Board in terms of control is a challenge in these circumstances. Competence, integrity, and commitment should go together. Although this shifts somewhat to a more remote guidance once a startup has transitioned to a scale-up, the attention point will still be valid.

It is the author's conviction that Corporate Governance when applied in such a way in startups and scale-ups is both a necessity and a blessing. A necessity because it will make sure regulatory and legal obligations are better respected; a blessing because if consistently applied and implemented, this Governance can substantially contribute to the company's success and even its survival. Corporate Governance is not a burden, it is a vector for proper strategy development and implementation.

The step in moving from a startup to a scale-up frequently involves new major investors stepping into the capital of the company. This implies a further shift in Corporate Governance to a higher level, without actually being completely different, obviously. With the growing complexity and dimensions of the company, Corporate Governance becomes even more important and the startups that have taken good Corporate Governance on board from day one will only reap the benefits of these efforts.

Finally: it is clear that even outstanding Corporate Governance cannot fully guarantee the success of a startup or a scale-up. But it will ensure the startup or scale-up does not fail because of failed Governance which is unfortunately still too frequently the case.

ADDENDA

Addendum 1: Director selection matrix

Addendum 2: BOD annual agenda model

Addendum 3: Financial reporting model

Addendum 4: Elements of legal and regulatory compliance

Addendum 5: Charter of the Board of Directors

Addendum 6: Steps Capital Increase

Addendum 7: Remuneration of Board members

Addendum 1
Director selection matrix

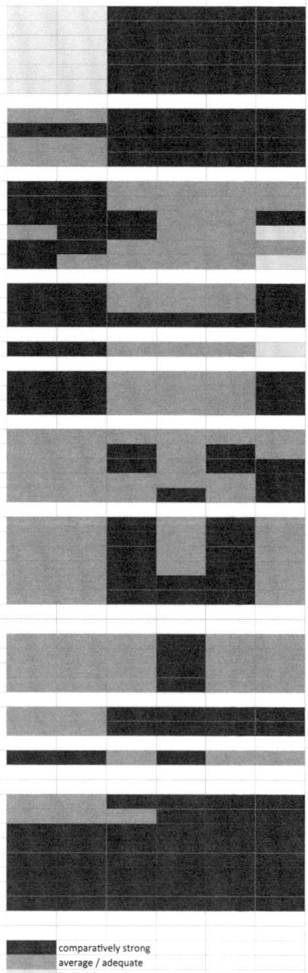

Board Competencies
DATE

Competencies	*Members*	A	B	C	D	E	F
1. Board experience							
General							
Specific for company							
Corporate Governance							
Legislation & regulations for Boards							
Board Committees							
2. Strategy / vision / mission							
Development							
Validation and follow-up							
Long-term dimension							
3. Company business knowledge							
Operations							
Business model / drivers							
R&D							
Marketing							
Communication & PR							
4. Company customers' knowledge							
Specific customer needs							
Business environment and evolution							
5. Company suppliers knowledge							
6. Company markets							
Relevant competitors							
Market evolution & drivers							
7. Company development							
Growth environment							
M&A							
IPO							
International dimension							
8. Finance & Administration							
Financing							
Accounting & Reporting							
Taxes, VAT etc.							
Risk definition & mitigation							
Investment evaluation & follow-up							
9. Human Resources							
Organization / structure							
People development							
Top management selection, compensation and development							
Internal communication							
10. Legal							
Compliance with applicable legislation							
11. ICT							
12. Specific director competencies							
Independence (for independent directors)							
Presidency (for chairman)							
Team player / dynamics / complementarity							
Ethics							
Availability							
Awareness of shareholders' interests							
Stakeholders' acquaintance							
Network impact							

Codes
- comparatively strong
- average / adequate
- limited / sporadic
- not defined / not applicable

Addendum 2
BOD annual agenda model

ABC NV

Board Meetings' Agendas, Sequence and Topics

Standard items for each Board meeting

- Approval of previous meeting minutes
- Review open actions lists
- Review of progress vs. targets and budget (HSEQ, commercial, operations + R&D, financials + cash flow, HR)
- Review ongoing projects

1. **Review of Y-1 (January–February)**
   - Review of (initial) performances vs. plan/budget of the preceding year
   - Additional items:
     - review HR issues
     - review financial positions / balance sheet

2. **Preparation of General Meeting (March–April)**
   - Approval of annual report of the BOD and review of the official accounting figures of Y-1 for approval by the general meeting
   - Setting of agenda for General Meeting
   - Additional items:
     - review risk management issues
     - link to insurances

3. **Continuous improvement and growth (May–June)**
   - Review all areas in which company operations can be improved, including elements such as
     - Legal obligations
     - Quality of delivery + HSE
   - Analyze growth opportunities and consolidate
   - Additional items:
     - review market position and customer feedback
     - analyze marketing and sales

4. **Opportunity meeting (July–August)**
   - Reflect on issues needing discussion, not covered in other meetings

5. **Review of long-term plan and vision (September–October)**
   - Actualize vision / mission if needed
   - Reflect on strategy and adapt if necessary
   - Investment needs and options
   - Additional items:
     - review development efforts
     - optimize structures

6. **Set Y + 1 plan and budget (November–December)**
   - Based on strategy and past experience, define targets plus milestones for Y + 1
   - Develop budget incl. P&L, balance sheet, cash flow projection, HR needs, additional items:
     - review tax and fiscal issues
     - review own performance

Addendum 3
Financial reporting model

FINANCIAL REPORTING MODEL k€

		Quarter actual (= last)	Quarter budget (plan)	Quarter Y-1 (pevious year)	YTD actual	YTD Budget (plan)	YTD Y-1 (previous year)	YE O/L	YE budget (plan)
Sales / Revenues / Turnover									
- Direct costs									
= Gross margin									
- Overhead costs									
= EBITDA									
- D&A									
= EBIT									
- I&T									
= Net Profit									

Notes

Quarter	Last reportable quarter (can be month also) - so Q1, Q2, Q3 or Q4
Y-1	Figure of the same periode in the previous year
Budget	Figure foreseen in the approved budget or plan of the year for the same period
YE	Year End = full year untill end of year
O/L	Outlook - best possible estimate based on actual and expected performance
Sales / Revenues / Turnover	All the invoiced sales plus possible other exceptional income (subsidies, compensations, ...)
Direct costs	Costs directly linked to sales
Overhead costs	All other costs not linked to sales (except for D&A, interest and taxes)
YTD	Year To Date figure since start of year

Addendum 4

Elements of legal and regulatory compliance

- Company law
  - Articles of association
    - Make sure your Corporate documents are in line with Belgian Corporate law. A new Belgian company code was introduced in May 2019. January 1, 2024, was the final date to take the necessary actions in front of the notary.
  - Obligations: company needs to take certain obligations into account, such:
    - (before incorporation) drafting a financial (business) plan;
    - maintaining a shareholders' register (to be consulted at the registered office);
    - holding an annual meeting of shareholders including an annual report; and
    - publishing the annual accounts;
    - specific actions in case of too low net assets (so-called alarm bell procedure);
    - etc.
- Relationship with the other shareholders (if any)

  When incorporating a company with multiple shareholders, it is highly advisable to make agreements beforehand with regard to votes, transfer of shares, exit, financing, etc.

  These agreements can be incorporated in the articles of association as well as in a shareholders' agreement.
- Tax and accounting law

  Depending on the activities of the company, the company must register with the VAT authorities and obtain a VAT-number. In this event, the company will i.a. have to file a VAT declaration every quarter as well as a VAT-listing of its clients every year.

- Social law
  - Depending on the size of the company, the company will have to take certain obligations into account such as:
    - registering with the social security services;
    - obtaining work permits;
    - drafting adequate working regulations;
    - taking into account working safety regulations;
    - holding social elections;
    - incorporating a committee for prevention and protection in the workplace;
    - etc.
  - Agreements with employees
    The company will have to ensure in labor agreements that are in line with social law. Points of attention are i.a.:
    - is there a collective labor agreement that must be taken into account?
    - noncompetition clauses are regulated;
    - pay-scale?
    - minimum number of holidays;
    - fringe benefits;
    - etc.
- Commercial law
  It is advisable to prepare template agreements such as:
  - general terms and conditions with regard to invoicing / delivery of goods / delivery of services;
  - customer agreements;
  - supplier agreements;
  - etc.
- Competition law such as cartel-related provisions (e.g., exchange of information): see the website of the Belgian Competition Authority for documentation on guidance (BMA/ABC). See also new legislation with regard to unlawful B2B contractual stipulations, abuse of economic dependency, and unfair market practices.

- Real estate
  - in the event the company owns or leases real estate, it needs to obtain a certain type of environmental permit depending on the activities of the company.
  - several other permits are obligatory, e.g., in the event the company wishes to hang a signboard;
  - in the event the company leases real estate, the lease agreement needs to be in compliance with the law. Some points of attention are:
    - nature of the agreement (commercial lease agreement vs. standard lease agreement);
    - registration of the lease agreement;
    - duration of the lease agreement (an agreement for more than nine (9) years needs to be entered into before a notary);
    - the duties of the lessor and lessee need to be specified and, according to the nature of the agreement, regulated;
    - etc.
- Specific compliance areas
  - some activities require additional permits and/or registration with the government. In Belgium, an overview can be found on this website: https://economie.fgov.be/nl/themas/ondernemingen/een-onderneming-oprichten/toegang-tot-het-beroep (only French or Dutch). Should you wish to perform the activities cross-border, then an overview of the specific regulations can be found here: https://ec.europa.eu/growth/tools-databases/regprof/
  - GDPR — Data protection
    Following the General Data Protection Regulation, companies need to adhere to certain measures in order to protect the privacy of the clients, employees, et al.
  - Health and safety regulations (see www.emploi.belgique.be and www.werk.belgie.be);

  - UBO register (register and declare, including annual update)
  - Permits (operational, environment, etc)
- IP / IT
  - make sure the trade name used by the company is unique and/or protected;
  - it is advisable to obtain patents, trademarks, copyrights, design, and model rights where applicable;
  - in the event the company wishes to play music in, e.g., a waiting room, it is obliged to pay a fee to SABAM (the Belgian Association of Authors, Composers, and Publishers).

Addendum 5
Charter of the Board of Directors

BOD's Charter

- The BOD is a group of professionals with the responsibility to direct (e.g., set vision / strategy etc.) and control (e.g., of operation / implementation / risks) the company in order to materialize the statutory objectives of the company as decided by the shareholders
- It operates as an independent collegial team, composed of complementary people working together in the best interest of the company
- The key values of the BOD are professionalism, transparency, ethics, confidentiality, trust, and sense of urgency
- The BOD subscribes fully to the principles of Corporate Governance
- A meeting of the BOD is documented in advance, prepared and reported
- The Chair of the BOD holds responsibility on the functioning of the BOD according to its Charter and responsibilities and functions as the representative of the BOD toward shareholders, management, and relevant outsiders
- Relationships with Management and Shareholders are structured, documented, and optimized; in particular, the BOD evaluates and structures top management
- The BOD will on a regular basis evaluate its efficiency, effectiveness, composition, and overall contribution to the results of the company

Approved by the BOD on ....

Chairman of the BOD

Addendum 6
Steps Capital Increase

- (Re-)agree on strategy
- Identify responsibilities: Who takes the lead ?
- Select M&A boutique (if appropriate)
- Make business and financial plan (including use of proceeds and cash flow)
- Mobilize legal and administrative support
- Produce teaser
- Identify type of investor desired
- Select investors willing to invest the needed amount (long list)
- Sign NDAs – NDAs
- Visit / meet potential investors
- Reduce to short list (3 to 5)
- Set up data room
- Collect LOIs
- Select best candidate
- Agree on basics of deal (valuation, participants, governance, exit, etc.) with new and existing shareholders
- Draft Term Sheet
- Execute DD and legal scan
- Agree on new shareholders' agreement and capital increase
- Write new articles of association and bylaws
- Special report accountant on valuation
- Special reports BOD
- Convert CLAs if required
- Fulfill conditions precedent
- Extraordinary shareholders' meeting (notarial deed)
- Payment and closing

Addendum 7
Remuneration of Board members

Company type *	Fixed annual payment €	Compensation per meeting attended €	Total annual compensation €
Micro	2500	500	4500
Small	4000	750	7000
Medium	8000	1000	12000
Bigger	10000	1250	15000

* Company type	Staff headcount	Turnover	or	Balance sheet total
Micro	< 10	≤ € 2 Mio		≤ € 2 Mio
Small	< 50	≤ € 10 Mio		≤ € 10 Mio
Medium	< 250	≤ € 50 Mio		≤ € 43 Mio
Bigger	> 250	> € 50 Mio		> € 43 Mio

Notes:

1. Source: Guberna recommendations 2012 (some form of indexation is recommended ...)
2. Chairman compensation: double the listed amounts
3. Additional compensation to be provided for Board committee memberships
4. Company type: EU SME definition

ABOUT THE AUTHOR

Luc Sterckx holds a MSc and a PhD in Chemical Engineering, as well as a post-graduate degree in Business Administration from Solvay business school and several other training certificates. He is equally a certified International Director from Insead.

He started his career with several years at Exxon, then became the startup CEO of Indaver before joining for a decade the executive committee of PetroFina (now Total), in which capacity he served as Managing Director of Fina Holding Deutschland and as Group Senior Vice President for all HSEQ matters worldwide. As the CEO he completed subsequently the MBO of Oleon and held after that the position of CEO of EDF-Luminus, the second largest power and gas company in Belgium.

He is currently an active Board member/president and company consultant in well over a dozen companies. Over a period of more than thirty years, he has sat on over thirty-five different Boards of Directors of various nature, structure, and origin—including listed companies, international boards, federations, and charity work. His director and counseling work focuses on the fields of energy and chemicals, environment, and corporate governance and he is involved in several startups as well as structured foundations and funds. He is a part-time Professor at KULeuven and an expert on internal governance. He is a Judge in Corporate Affairs and a Fellow of the International Academy of Management.

Luc Sterckx combines general management expertise in a very wide range of companies complexities / sizes, including mergers and acquisitions, startups, and turnarounds Judge in Corporate Affairs with a hands-on practical approach. He has particular strengths in corporate governance, both locally and internationally in a variety of Boards.